Disclaimer and/or Legal Notices:

While every attempt has been made to verify the information provided in this publication, neither the Author nor the Publisher assumes any responsibility for errors, omissions, or contrary interpretation of the subject matter herein. This publication is not intended for use as a source of legal or agricultural advice. The Publisher wants to stress that the information contained herein may be subject to varying state and/or local laws or regulations. All users are advised to retain competent counsel to determine what state and/or local laws or regulations may apply to the user's particular gardening activities.

The Purchaser or Reader of this publication assumes responsibility for the use of these materials and information. Adherence to all applicable laws and regulations, federal, state, and local, governing professional licensing, business practices, advertising, and all other aspects of doing business in the United States or any other jurisdiction is the sole responsibility of the Purchaser or Reader. The Author and Publisher assume no responsibility or liability whatsoever on the behalf of any Purchaser or Reader of these materials. Any perceived slights of specific people or organizations are unintentional.

The gardening techniques, tips, and other information presented in this book are for educational and informational purposes only. They are not intended as a substitute for professional agricultural or horticultural advice. Use of the gardening practices or approaches described in this publication should not replace professional consultation for land use or plant cultivation.

The reader should be aware that the efficacy and safety of gardening practices may vary based on environmental conditions, plant species, and individual care. It is crucial to research and understand any potential challenges or requirements before implementing any of the methods, designs, or techniques outlined in this book.

The author and publisher assume no liability for any adverse effects or consequences resulting from the use of the information presented in this book. The reader should use their own judgment and discretion in implementing any of the information provided in this book. Ultimately, it is the reader's responsibility to ensure that they are engaging in safe and effective gardening practices. It is important for readers to conduct their own thorough research and consult with a qualified professional before embarking on any significant gardening projects. The author and publisher are not responsible for any adverse effects or consequences resulting from the use of the information presented in this book.

BONUS! FREE GARDENING CALENDAR

We're thrilled to offer our buyers a special bonus: the Gardening Planner, an invaluable tool to accompany "Gardening Secrets of Our Ancestors." This comprehensive planner is designed to help gardeners of all levels stay organized and maximize their gardening efforts throughout the year. With sections for yearly, monthly, and daily planning, you can keep track of every aspect of your garden, from planting schedules to harvest logs.

The Gardening Planner includes detailed plant care profiles, allowing you to document essential information for each plant, such as watering schedules, repotting frequencies, and specific care instructions. It also features sections for seed inventory, garden equipment lists, and expense logs, ensuring that you have a complete overview of your gardening resources and expenditures. Additionally, the planner offers templates for garden layouts, companion planting charts, and seasonal checklists, helping you plan and maintain a thriving garden all year round. Use this planner to track your successes, learn from challenges, and make informed decisions for future gardening seasons.

Scan the QR code below or visit https://ezlinkshare.com/of5s to access your free gardening planner book.

INTRODUCTION

Hello and welcome to a journey through the garden gates of history. My name is Jill Brady, and I'm delighted to guide you down the meandering paths of ancient wisdom with our new book, "Gardening Secrets of Our Ancestors." Gardening is not just my profession but a passion deeply rooted in my family's way of life. Alongside my husband, Dan, I've cultivated not just crops, but a lifestyle that thrives on the self-reliant, hearty ethos of homesteading.

Living off-the-grid in the countryside, our home is a vibrant tableau of lush vegetable plots and fragrant herb gardens, underscored by the rhythmic sounds of nature and the occasional clatter from Dan's woodworking shop. Here, we've shaped a world where each day is a testament to living simply and sustainably.

Gardening is more than just planting seeds for us. It's about connecting with the earth, understanding its rhythms, and using that knowledge to nourish not only our bodies but also our souls. Over the years, I've honed the art of canning, preserving the bounty of our garden through seasons, and sharing this abundance at local farmers' markets. These experiences have imbued me with invaluable insights—secrets that have been passed down through generations, yet somehow forgotten in the modern hustle.

In "Gardening Secrets of Our Ancestors," we will delve into over 200 of these forgotten secrets. This book isn't a mere how-to guide; it's an invitation to weave the threads of past wisdom into the fabric of your garden, creating a tapestry that is both productive and sustainable. Whether you're a novice with a budding interest or a seasoned gardener with dirt-caked gloves, the insights shared here aim to enrich your gardening practice, reduce frustrations, and maximize your harvests.

As we turn these pages together, we'll rediscover age-old techniques that once filled the storehouses and larders of our forebearers with plenty, exploring everything from the layout of ancestral garden plots to the natural remedies that kept their plants thriving. So, grab your gardening tools and let's dig into the past to sow the seeds for a more fruitful future.

The Purpose of this Book

In an age where convenience often dictates our choices, the art of gardening has seen a shift towards quick fixes and store-bought solutions. Many gardeners, both seasoned and new, might dash off to the nearest Home Depot or Lowe's at the first sign of a gardening predicament. While these modern conveniences offer immediate gratification and apparent ease, they frequently come laden with chemicals and practices that stray far from the natural processes our gardens thrive on.

This book aims to steer us back to the roots of traditional gardening, where the rhythms of nature were respected and leveraged to create bountiful harvests. The wisdom compiled here is drawn from a time when gardeners turned to their surroundings to solve problems, using methods that were not only effective but also safe and sustainable. These practices were not just about solving immediate issues but about fostering a thriving garden ecosystem that could sustain itself and its keepers over many seasons.

Our ancestors understood the delicate balance required in gardens long before "organic" became a buzzword. They cultivated their plots with a deep knowledge of how each element interacts within the garden ecosystem. From companion planting to natural pest repellents, their techniques were developed through observation and experience, devoid of synthetic chemicals that might harm the environment or our health.

The goal of this book is to reconnect today's gardeners with this timeless wisdom, providing them with knowledge that can minimize reliance on unsafe and untested chemicals. As someone who tends her own garden with the aim of keeping my family's health and well-being at the forefront, I understand the importance of using methods that enhance both the quality and safety of our produce. This isn't just about nostalgia; it's about a practical, proven approach to gardening that respects both our health and that of the planet.

By embracing the techniques in this book, you will learn how to address common gardening challenges using solutions that have nourished generations. Whether it's reviving depleted soil with natural amendments, managing pests through age-old companion planting strategies, or designing a garden that naturally enhances plant health and productivity, the secrets shared here will help you cultivate a garden that is not only abundant but also inherently safe and sustainable. Let's embark on this journey together, drawing on the wisdom of the past to nurture a healthier future for our gardens and families.

Traditional Gardening Wisdom

My journey into the depths of gardening wisdom began in the soil of my grandparents' backyard, under the watchful eyes of towering sunflowers and amidst the sweet aroma of ripening tomatoes. It was there, in the early dawn with dew still fresh upon the earth, that I first learned to turn the soil and plant seeds with careful, hopeful fingers. My grandparents, who had inherited their green fingers from generations before them, taught me not just how to garden, but how to connect with the land and listen to its subtle teachings.

These lessons weren't confined to mere horticultural techniques; they were imbued with stories of old, of survival and resilience, of the Great Depression and wars, when gardens were more than just a hobby—they were a lifeline. Every plant, every technique had a story, a legacy that stretched back through decades. This oral tradition of passing down knowledge is the bedrock upon which this book is founded.

As I grew and took these teachings to heart, my passion for gardening blossomed into a vocation. Selling our produce at local farmers' markets not only became a way to share the fruits of our labor but also a rich avenue for exchange of knowledge with other gardeners and farmers. These markets are a treasure trove of living history, where each vendor carries forward the legacy of their own ancestral wisdom. It is here among the colorful stalls, while exchanging tales and tips over crates of fresh harvest, that I find myself constantly enlightened by "aha" moments.

These revelations are often simple, yet profoundly effective strategies—like planting marigolds to deter pests, or using leaf mold for enriching the soil—techniques that many might consider outdated but are, in fact, testament to a time when gardeners were masterful observers of nature. Each week brings a new piece of this nearly forgotten wisdom, and every piece is a reminder of how much more there is to learn.

"Gardening Secrets of Our Ancestors" is therefore more than just a personal narrative; it is a collective chronicle of generations of gardeners. This book stitches together a patchwork of experiences—mine, my grandparents', and those of fellow gardeners—to present a comprehensive guide filled with wisdom that has stood the test of time. It's a compilation that honors the past while serving the present, ensuring that these precious insights continue to enrich our gardening practices and reconnect us with the natural world. As we turn each page, we revive the traditions that have nourished our ancestors and continue to empower modern gardeners with sustainable, effective practices that are as beneficial today as they were a hundred years ago.

Now that you understand the roots from which this invaluable wisdom has sprung, and the paths through which it has been gathered, we are poised to delve into the very heart of what brought you here. With a rich tapestry of traditional knowledge at our fingertips, let's roll up our sleeves and unearth the practical, time-tested secrets that make up the essence of this book. Ready to get into the nitty-gritty? Let's begin our journey into the verdant past, to cultivate a bountiful future.

CHAPTER 1: GARDEN PLANNING & DESIGN

Planning and designing a garden is an art form that marries functionality with aesthetic beauty, incorporating age-old wisdom into every aspect. This chapter unveils secrets like using bleach for tool maintenance and vinegar for rust removal, which ensure your gardening tools are both effective and long-lasting. We'll explore how color coordination can enhance the visual appeal of your garden and how planting lavender attracts vital pollinators.

Additionally, we'll discuss optimal spacing to maximize plant health and production, and the unique use of yogurt to encourage natural moss growth, adding an old-world charm to garden features. Each tip not only beautifies your space but also fortifies its sustainability, echoing gardening traditions that have stood the test of time. Let's dive into these practical yet transformative strategies to cultivate a thriving, enchanting garden.

Bleach For Tool Maintenance

Bleach is not just a staple for household cleaning; it plays a crucial role in garden tool maintenance as well. Diluting bleach with water creates an effective solution for cleaning garden tools, an essential practice for preventing the spread of plant diseases. As you prune, cut, or dig, your tools come into contact with various plant materials, potentially collecting pathogens that can lead to disease outbreaks. By regularly sterilizing your tools with a bleach solution, you ensure that they remain not only visibly clean but also free from microbial threats. This simple practice keeps your garden healthy and safeguards the well-being of every plant in your care.

Garden Color Coordination

Garden color coordination goes beyond mere aesthetics; it is a strategic approach that enhances the visual impact of your garden while also attracting beneficial pollinators. By thoughtfully planning the color palette of your garden, you can create a vibrant display that is not only pleasing to the eye but also conducive to the health of your garden. Colors like bright yellows, deep blues, and rich purples are particularly effective at drawing in bees, butterflies, and other pollinators that play a critical role in the success of your garden. Such planning ensures that your garden is not only a feast for the eyes but a bustling habitat for essential wildlife, contributing to a robust and flourishing ecosystem.

Lavender to Attract Pollinators

Planting lavender in your garden serves as a dual-purpose strategy that boosts both beauty and biodiversity. Lavender's vibrant purple blooms and soothing fragrance make it a standout addition, enhancing the garden's aesthetic appeal. More importantly, these flowers are highly attractive to bees and butterflies, key pollinators vital for successful plant reproduction. By incorporating lavender, you not only enrich the visual tapestry of your space but also support a thriving pollination process, essential for a healthy and productive garden.

Optimal Spacing

Optimal spacing in your garden is crucial for maximizing plant health and growth. By giving each plant ample room, you minimize competition for essential resources like sunlight, water, and nutrients. This spacing allows each plant to flourish without being overshadowed or choked by its neighbors, ensuring better air circulation and reducing the risk of disease transmission. Thoughtful spacing not only leads to healthier plants but also significantly enhances overall garden productivity, allowing each plant to reach its full potential.

Vinegar to Clean Garden Tools

Using vinegar to clean rusty garden tools is an eco-friendly method that not only restores the tools but also extends their life. The natural acidic properties of vinegar effectively break down rust, allowing you to salvage and rejuvenate tools that may seem beyond repair. This simple, non-toxic approach not only saves you money on replacements but also reduces waste, contributing to a more sustainable gardening practice. Regularly treating your tools with vinegar not only keeps them in optimal condition but also ensures they remain effective and safe to use, helping maintain the overall health and beauty of your garden.

White Vinegar for Cleaning Pots

White vinegar is an excellent choice for cleaning and disinfecting plant pots and containers. Its acidic nature effectively removes unsightly mold and stubborn mineral deposits that can accumulate over time. Using white vinegar not only ensures that your containers are spotless but also prevents potential pathogens and contaminants from affecting your plants. This method is especially beneficial for gardeners looking to reuse pots each season, providing a clean and sterile environment that promotes healthy plant growth. Simple and environmentally friendly, this cleaning technique keeps your gardening practices safe and sustainable.

Yogurt for Moss

Using yogurt to encourage moss growth on shady stones or concrete surfaces is a delightful trick to add a touch of whimsy and natural beauty to your garden. The live cultures in yogurt act as a catalyst, promoting the growth of moss in areas where it might not naturally colonize. By simply spreading a thin layer of plain yogurt on these surfaces, you create a conducive environment for moss to thrive. This technique is particularly effective in shaded garden nooks, where moss can enhance the aesthetic appeal with its soft, green carpet, blending seamlessly into the landscape and adding an ancient, woodland feel to your garden spaces.

CHAPTER 2: FERTILIZATION & SOIL HEALTH

Proper soil health is essential for a thriving garden, serving as the foundation for all plant growth. This chapter delves into the essential principles of soil fertility and the time-honored methods for enhancing it. We'll explore a range of organic amendments that enrich the soil naturally—such as burying fish scraps, incorporating coffee grounds, and adding banana peels. These practices not only boost nutrient levels but also improve soil structure and water retention.

Adopting these traditional techniques can significantly enhance your garden's productivity. By integrating methods like using biochar, green manures, and effective composting, you create a vibrant, self-sustaining ecosystem. These strategies not only echo the sustainable practices of our ancestors but also promise a fertile garden capable of yielding abundant harvests year after year.

Alfalfa Meal to Boost Roses

Alfalfa meal is an excellent natural booster for roses, enriching them with nitrogen and essential minerals that promote lush foliage and vibrant blooms. The triacontanol in alfalfa enhances photosynthesis and root development, leading to healthier, more robust plants. When mixed into the soil as a slow-release fertilizer, alfalfa meal not only feeds the roses but also improves soil structure, ensuring better aeration and drainage for optimal rose health and beauty.

Ammonia for Nitrogen Boost

Ammonia is an effective nitrogen source that can quickly invigorate plant growth, particularly useful in nitrogen-deficient soils. When diluted and applied as a foliar spray or directly to the soil, ammonia breaks down, releasing nitrogen that plants can immediately absorb. This rapid infusion of nitrogen helps promote vigorous leaf growth and greening, essential for photosynthesis and overall plant health. However, it's important to use ammonia sparingly and carefully, as over-application can harm plant roots and soil microbiology. Always ensure proper dilution and application techniques to safely harness the benefits of ammonia for your garden.

Baking Soda as a pH Neutralizer

Baking soda is a versatile and gentle option for gardeners looking to adjust soil pH towards a more neutral level. Particularly useful in acidic soils, baking soda can help raise the pH, making the environment more hospitable for plants that prefer neutral to slightly alkaline conditions. By sprinkling a small amount of baking soda around the soil and watering it in, you can effectively neutralize acidic conditions. This adjustment helps improve nutrient availability, promoting healthier plant growth and vigor. However, it's crucial to apply baking soda in moderation and to test soil pH before and after application to avoid overly alkalizing the soil.

Baking Soda for Sweeter Tomatoes

Baking soda can be a simple, natural method to sweeten the taste of your tomatoes. By lightly sprinkling baking soda on the soil around your tomato plants—not on the plants themselves—you can subtly raise the soil's pH, reducing acidity. This adjustment encourages the tomatoes to develop a sweeter flavor. The baking soda helps moderate the soil environment, which influences the acidity levels in the tomatoes as they grow. However, it's important to use this technique sparingly and to monitor the soil's pH closely to ensure it remains within a healthy range for tomato plants, as too much alkalinity can adversely affect overall plant health.

Banana Peel in Planting Hole

Placing banana peels in the planting holes of your garden plants is a natural, effective way to enrich the soil with essential nutrients. Banana peels are rich in potassium, phosphorus, and calcium, which are crucial for healthy plant growth, flower development, and fruiting. By cutting up a banana peel and placing it at the bottom of a planting hole or burying it near the roots of existing plants, you provide a slow-release fertilizer that feeds the plants as it decomposes. This method not only boosts plant health and vigor but also improves soil quality and reduces waste, contributing to a more sustainable gardening practice.

Banana Peel Potassium Boost

Banana peels are an excellent source of potassium, an essential nutrient that plays a critical role in plant health and development. Incorporating banana peels into your garden soil can naturally enhance potassium levels, which helps in strengthening plant cell walls, improving overall sturdiness and drought resistance. Additionally, potassium is vital for the proper functioning of plant processes, including photosynthesis and enzyme activation, which contribute to vigorous growth and more abundant fruit production. Simply chop up banana peels and bury them in the soil around your plants to provide a gradual, natural potassium boost that will encourage healthier, more resilient plants.

Banana Peel Water

Banana peel water is a simple, sustainable way to provide your plants with a nutrient-rich boost. To make this natural fertilizer, soak banana peels in a jar of water for a few days, allowing the nutrients to leach out into the water. This infused water is particularly high in potassium, phosphorus, and calcium—key elements that support plant growth, flowering, and fruit development. Use this banana peel water to hydrate your plants, giving them a gentle, effective nutrient boost with each watering. This method not only utilizes kitchen scraps that might otherwise go to waste but also encourages a more organic approach to gardening, enhancing plant health and vitality without chemical fertilizers.

Beer for Fertilizer

Using beer as a fertilizer in the garden is an unconventional yet effective method for nourishing plants. Beer is rich in yeast and carbohydrates, which promote beneficial microbial activity in the soil. These microbes enhance soil health by breaking down organic matter and releasing nutrients that are readily available to plants. Pouring diluted beer around the base of your plants can help improve soil structure, increase nutrient uptake, and boost plant growth. However, it's important to use this method sparingly, as excessive use can attract unwanted pests. A light application can invigorate your plants and enrich your soil, making beer a resourceful addition to your gardening practices.

Bury Fish Scraps for Fertilizer

Burying fish scraps in the garden is a time-honored method to enrich the soil with nutrients that promote plant health and vigorous growth. Fish scraps are rich in nitrogen, phosphorus, and other essential nutrients that plants require to thrive. By digging a hole about 8-12 inches deep away from the base of the plant (to prevent root damage and deter scavengers), and burying the fish scraps, you can create a natural, slow-release fertilizer. As the fish decomposes, it gradually releases these nutrients into the soil, enhancing its fertility and improving plant vitality. This method is particularly beneficial for nutrient-hungry plants like tomatoes and corn, boosting their growth significantly.

Calcium for Fruit Firmness

Calcium plays a crucial role in the garden, particularly in enhancing fruit firmness and quality. This essential nutrient helps in the formation of plant cell walls, leading to stronger, more robust plant tissues. For fruiting plants, adequate calcium intake is vital to prevent disorders such as blossom end rot in tomatoes and peppers, which occurs when there is a calcium deficiency. Adding calcium to the soil, whether through lime, gypsum, or even crushed eggshells, can significantly improve the structural integrity and storability of the fruits, ensuring they are firm and less prone to damage during growth and after harvest. Regularly supplementing your garden soil with calcium will encourage healthier, more resilient fruit production, leading to a more successful harvest.

Coffee Grounds for Acid-Lovers

Coffee grounds are an excellent addition to the garden, especially for acid-loving plants like azaleas, blueberries, and rhododendrons. These grounds are naturally acidic and can help lower the pH of the soil, creating an ideal environment for these types of plants to thrive. Incorporating coffee grounds into the soil around acid-loving plants provides them with a mild, consistent source of acidity as well as essential nutrients such as nitrogen, which is slowly released as the grounds decompose. This not only enriches the soil but also enhances leaf coloration and bloom production, promoting overall plant health and vigor.

Coffee Grounds for Nitrogen Boost

Coffee grounds are a valuable source of nitrogen, making them an excellent amendment for enriching garden soil. As coffee grounds decompose, they release nitrogen, a critical nutrient that supports leafy growth and the overall green vigor of plants. Incorporating used coffee grounds into the soil or adding them to your compost pile can boost the nitrogen content, which is particularly beneficial for growing vegetables and other nitrogen-hungry plants. This sustainable practice not only recycles waste but also enhances soil fertility naturally, supporting robust plant development and a healthier garden ecosystem.

Compost Tea Feedings

Compost tea is a nutrient-rich liquid made by steeping compost in water, which can be used to feed plants, providing a quick, easily absorbable boost of nutrients. This method effectively extracts beneficial microorganisms and soluble nutrients from compost, creating a potent liquid fertilizer that enhances plant growth and soil health. Applying compost tea to both the soil and the foliage of plants helps to suppress diseases, promote vigorous growth, and improve nutrient uptake. Regular feedings with compost tea invigorate the microbial activity in the soil, fostering a more dynamic, healthy garden environment. This sustainable practice not only maximizes the utility of your compost but also ensures your plants receive a balanced, gentle infusion of essential nutrients.

Cooking Water for Plant Nutrition

Using cooking water to nourish plants is an efficient and resourceful way of recycling nutrients. When you boil or steam vegetables, the water absorbs minerals and vitamins released from the food. Instead of discarding this nutrient-rich water, let it cool and then use it to water your plants. This provides them with a variety of dissolved nutrients, such as calcium, magnesium, and potassium, which can enhance plant growth and vitality. This method is particularly useful for houseplants or garden vegetables, offering a simple yet effective supplement to regular watering routines. By reusing cooking water, you reduce waste and give your plants an extra nutritional boost.

Eggshell Water for Plants

Eggshell water is an excellent homemade fertilizer that can help strengthen and nourish your plants. Rich in calcium, eggshells can enhance plant cell wall structure, leading to healthier and more robust plants. To make eggshell water, simply rinse and crush eggshells, then soak them in a jar of water for a few days, allowing the calcium to leach into the water. This eggshell-infused water can be used to irrigate plants, providing them with a steady supply of calcium. This is particularly beneficial for preventing blossom end rot in tomatoes and peppers and promoting overall plant health. Using eggshell water is a fantastic way to recycle kitchen waste while enriching your plants with essential nutrients.

Epsom Salt Fertilizer

Epsom salt, chemically known as magnesium sulfate, is a valuable addition to the garden, particularly as a fertilizer. Magnesium is crucial for plant photosynthesis, and sulfur is important for plant protein production and enzyme activities. Epsom salt can be dissolved in water and used to feed plants, promoting healthier foliage, brighter flowers, and increased fruit production. This solution is especially beneficial for plants suffering from magnesium deficiency, evident from yellowing leaves between the veins. Applying Epsom salt to plants like tomatoes, peppers, and roses can boost their growth and vitality significantly. It can also help improve flower blooming and enhances a plant's green color. A periodic application of Epsom salt water can ensure your plants receive these essential nutrients in an easily absorbable form, leading to lush, vibrant growth.

Gypsum for Soil Improvement

Gypsum, a naturally occurring mineral made of calcium sulfate, is effective for improving soil structure, especially in clay and heavy soils. It works by breaking up compacted soil, which enhances water penetration and root growth. This improvement allows for better drainage and aeration, vital for healthy roots. Gypsum also provides essential nutrients like calcium and sulfur but does not alter soil pH, making it ideal for maintaining the current pH balance while improving soil conditions. Regular applications can lead to more vigorous plant growth and increased soil fertility over time.

Iced Tea for Acidic Soil Plants

Iced tea can be a resourceful way to water plants that thrive in acidic soil conditions. As tea is naturally acidic, using leftover unsweetened iced tea to water acid-loving plants like azaleas, rhododendrons, and blueberries can help maintain the acidic pH levels these plants prefer. The tannic acid in tea adds mild acidity to the soil, which can enhance nutrient uptake and improve overall plant health. This method is not only a great way to use up leftover iced tea but also supports the growth and vibrancy of your acidophilic garden plants, fostering a more suitable environment for their thriving.

Mycorrhizal Inoculants

Mycorrhizal inoculants are beneficial fungi that form symbiotic relationships with plant roots, significantly enhancing plant health and soil vitality. These fungi extend the roots' reach, enabling better access to nutrients and water, which boosts plant growth and resilience against environmental stresses. Applying mycorrhizal inoculants is especially advantageous when establishing new plants, as it helps them adapt and thrive in new environments. This improved nutrient uptake not only increases plant yield and health but also enhances soil structure and fertility. Incorporating mycorrhizal fungi into gardening practices fosters a healthier, more biodiverse soil ecosystem, supporting a more productive and sustainable garden.

Oatmeal to Boost Plant Growth

Oatmeal is a natural and effective way to boost plant growth by enriching the soil with essential nutrients. As a good source of phosphorus and iron, oatmeal, when added to garden soil, gradually decomposes and releases these vital minerals. This not only promotes healthy root development but also enhances overall plant vigor and growth. Oatmeal also acts as a food source for beneficial soil microbes, which improve soil structure and health. By sprinkling dry oatmeal around the base of plants or mixing it into the soil during planting, gardeners can ensure their plants receive a steady infusion of nutrients, fostering stronger and more resilient growth.

Pine Needle Mulch for Blueberries

Pine needle mulch is an excellent choice for blueberry bushes, as it naturally helps maintain the acidic soil conditions that blueberries thrive in. The pine needles slowly break down and contribute to a lower pH level, which enhances nutrient availability, particularly iron, a crucial element for blueberries. Additionally, pine needle mulch helps conserve soil moisture, suppresses weed growth, and adds organic matter to the soil as it decomposes. The mulch also creates a clean and visually appealing ground cover around the plants, reducing the risk of fruit rot by preventing berries from touching the damp soil directly. Using pine needle mulch for blueberries not only improves their growth and fruit production but also supports overall plant health in an environmentally friendly way.

Potato Peel as Rose Fertilizer

Potato peels can serve as an excellent organic fertilizer for rose bushes, providing them with essential nutrients to enhance growth and bloom quality. Rich in potassium, which is crucial for flower development and overall plant health, potato peels help strengthen the plant's cell walls, improve resistance to disease, and aid in water regulation within the plant. To utilize potato peels as fertilizer, simply bury them shallowly around the base of your rose plants. As the peels decompose, they slowly release nutrients into the soil, enriching it and feeding your roses. This method is not only sustainable, reducing kitchen waste, but also promotes a more natural, chemical-free approach to nurturing your garden's spectacular blooms.

Potato Water for Iron

Potato water, the water left over from boiling potatoes, is a resourceful way to add iron to your garden soil. Potatoes naturally contain iron, and some of these mineral leaches into the water during cooking. By using cooled potato water to irrigate your plants, you can provide them with an additional source of iron, which is essential for promoting healthy plant growth and enhancing chlorophyll production. This is particularly beneficial for plants showing signs of iron deficiency, often indicated by yellowing leaves with green veins. Utilizing potato water not only maximizes the use of kitchen waste but also supports plant health in a natural and eco-friendly manner.

Powdered Milk for Calcium & Soil Amendment

Powdered milk serves as a versatile soil amendment, providing a rich source of calcium and other beneficial nutrients to enhance plant health. When added to the soil, powdered milk slowly releases calcium, crucial for strengthening plant cell walls and preventing disorders like blossom end rot in tomatoes and peppers. It also boosts the overall soil ecosystem by promoting the growth of beneficial bacteria, which improve nutrient absorption and soil structure. To incorporate powdered milk into your garden, you can sprinkle it directly onto the soil around your plants or dissolve it in water to create a nourishing solution for regular watering. This method not only ensures that your plants receive vital nutrients but also helps maintain a balanced and productive soil environment.

Rice Water for Fertilizer

Rice water, the starchy liquid left over after rinsing or boiling rice, is a nutrient-rich resource for garden plants. This water contains vitamins and minerals leached from the rice, which can act as a mild fertilizer. It also has starches that encourage beneficial bacteria and fungi in the soil, enhancing soil health and structure. Using rice water in your garden is simple: allow it to cool after cooking and use it to water your plants. This practice not only helps in recycling kitchen waste but also provides a sustainable way to boost plant growth and vitality without the use of chemical fertilizers. Regular use of rice water can improve plant resilience and promote healthier, more vigorous growth.

Stinging Nettle Fertilizer

Stinging nettle serves as an excellent natural fertilizer due to its richness in vital nutrients like nitrogen, iron, magnesium, and sulfur. To harness these benefits, you can create nettle tea by soaking the leaves and stems in water for a few weeks, allowing them to ferment and release nutrients into the water. This potent liquid, known as nettle tea, can be diluted with water at a ratio of 1:10 and used to water plants or as a foliar feed. Nettle tea not only promotes strong, healthy growth and increases resistance to pests and diseases but also activates soil bacteria, enhancing soil structure and fertility. This method recycles waste while naturally boosting garden health.

Tea Bags as Fertilizer

Used tea bags can be an effective and eco-friendly fertilizer for your garden, providing a subtle boost in nutrients. Tea leaves contain nitrogen, potassium, and phosphorus, essential elements for plant growth. Additionally, the slight acidity of tea is beneficial for acid-loving plants such as roses, azaleas, and blueberries. To utilize tea bags as fertilizer, simply cut them open and sprinkle the damp leaves around the base of your plants. The tea leaves decompose gradually, enriching the soil with organic matter and nutrients. This method not only nourishes your plants but also helps to improve soil structure and moisture retention, promoting healthier plant growth while repurposing your kitchen waste.

Used Coffee Filter Compost

Used coffee filters and the grounds they contain are excellent additions to compost piles, enriching them with essential nutrients. The filters, typically made from natural, biodegradable paper, break down easily, while the nitrogen-rich coffee grounds help balance the carbon-to-nitrogen ratio crucial for effective composting. Simply toss both into your compost bin where the grounds will aerate the pile and attract beneficial earthworms. This method efficiently recycles kitchen waste, enhances compost quality, and produces a rich, nutritious soil amendment that significantly benefits garden plants.

Vegetable Stock from Scraps

Creating vegetable stock from kitchen scraps not only reduces waste but also repurposes vegetable trimmings like carrot peels, onion ends, and unused portions of celery and herbs. Simmer these scraps in water to extract flavors and nutrients, producing a rich homemade stock. After straining the stock for culinary use, add the softened vegetable remnants to your compost bin. These nutrient-rich scraps will decompose and enrich the compost with minerals and organic matter, enhancing the fertility of your garden soil. This method efficiently turns kitchen waste into a valuable resource for both your cooking and gardening endeavors, promoting a sustainable cycle of reuse.

Vinegar as an Acid Enhancer

Vinegar can be used effectively in the garden to lower soil pH, making it an excellent acid enhancer for plants that thrive in more acidic conditions, such as blueberries, azaleas, and gardenias. By diluting vinegar with water (typically one cup of vinegar to a gallon of water), you can create a solution that, when applied to the soil, helps increase its acidity. This adjustment can improve the availability of certain nutrients that are more soluble in acidic environments, enhancing plant health and growth. However, it's important to use this method sparingly and to monitor soil pH levels regularly, as too much acidity can harm plants. Vinegar is a readily available and cost-effective tool for gardeners needing to manage soil acidity naturally.

Whey from Yogurt as Fertilizer

Whey, the liquid byproduct of yogurt, is an excellent natural fertilizer due to its rich content of proteins and minerals, particularly potassium and phosphorus. When used in the garden, whey can improve plant growth by providing these essential nutrients. It also introduces beneficial bacteria to the soil, enhancing soil health and helping plants absorb nutrients more effectively. To use whey as a fertilizer, dilute it with water—about one part whey to ten parts water—to prevent it from being too strong for plants, which could potentially burn their roots. This diluted whey solution can then be applied directly to the soil around the plants. Utilizing whey not only recycles a kitchen byproduct but also supports a healthier, more productive garden.

Worm Tea Fertilizer

Worm tea, an extract made from the liquid drained from a worm composting bin, is a potent natural fertilizer that offers numerous benefits to the garden. Rich in beneficial microbes and nutrients like nitrogen, phosphorus, and potassium, worm tea helps enhance soil health, promotes vigorous plant growth, and increases resistance to disease. To create worm tea, simply collect the liquid that naturally seeps from the bottom of a worm bin, or steep worm castings in water. This solution can be diluted and used as a foliar spray or soil drench, effectively boosting nutrient absorption and encouraging beneficial microbial activity in the soil. Regular applications of worm tea can lead to healthier, more resilient plants, making it an invaluable addition to any organic gardening regimen.

More Fertilization & Soil Health Secrets

Secret	Why It Works	What to Do
Molasses Fertilizer	Provides a source of sugars that feed beneficial soil microbes, enhancing soil health and plant growth.	Dissolve a tablespoon of molasses in a gallon of water and use it to water plants.
Seaweed Extract	Rich in micronutrients, promotes root growth, increases resistance to pests and diseases.	Use liquid seaweed extract as a foliar spray or soil drench.
Humic Acid	Enhances soil structure, increases water retention, and improves nutrient availability.	Apply humic acid to soil to improve nutrient uptake.
Wood Ash	Adds potassium and lime, helps to raise soil pH for acidic soils.	Sprinkle wood ash lightly over garden beds.
Fish Emulsion	Provides a quick-acting source of nitrogen and trace minerals.	Dilute fish emulsion with water and use as a soil drench or foliar spray.
Gelatin for Nitrogen	Supplies nitrogen to support leafy growth.	Dissolve unflavored gelatin in water and use it to water plants.
Epsom Salt Spray	Provides magnesium and sulfur, promotes greener foliage and improved flowering.	Mix 1 tablespoon of Epsom salt in a gallon of water and spray on plant leaves.
Green Manure	Adds organic matter, fixes nitrogen, and improves soil structure.	Grow cover crops such as clover, vetch, or rye and turn them into the soil before planting.
Blood Meal	Promotes rapid plant growth, especially useful for leafy vegetables.	Apply blood meal to soil as a nitrogen-rich fertilizer.
Bat Guano	High in nitrogen, phosphorus, and potassium, enhances plant vigor and flowering.	Mix bat guano into the soil or brew it into a tea for watering.
Alfalfa Pellets	Provides nitrogen, phosphorus, and beneficial growth hormones.	Mix alfalfa pellets into the soil before planting.
Azomite	Improves overall plant health and soil fertility.	Add azomite to soil to replenish trace minerals.
Biochar	Enhances soil structure, increases water and nutrient retention, and supports beneficial microbial activity.	Incorporate biochar into the soil.
Comfrey Tea	High in potassium, promotes flowering and fruiting.	Soak comfrey leaves in water for several weeks to create a nutrient-rich liquid fertilizer.

CHAPTER 3: COMPANION GARDENING

Companion gardening taps into the natural synergies between different plant species, optimizing space use while enhancing plant health and productivity through ecological means. Understanding the specific benefits of planting certain species together allows gardeners to naturally deter pests, improve pollination, and boost crop yields. For example, planting basil with tomatoes not only conserves garden space but also helps enhance the flavor and growth of the tomatoes, showcasing how companion planting promotes mutual benefits among garden species.

This approach includes various effective pairings such as chamomile, which boosts seed germination, and chives, which prevent apple scab. Corn, when planted near squash, provides necessary shade that fosters a beneficial microclimate for growth, while dill attracts beneficial insects that serve as natural pest control. Lemon balm is excellent for drawing bees, crucial for pollination, whereas nasturtiums act as a trap crop for aphids, protecting more vulnerable plants. Strategic combinations like onions and carrots help repel pests that target each, and radishes near cucumbers can ward off cucumber beetles. Each pairing underscores the ecological and practical advantages of companion gardening, enhancing the success and sustainability of garden ecosystems.

Basil and Tomato Synergy

Growing basil near tomatoes is a classic example of companion planting that offers multiple benefits. The presence of basil has been shown to enhance the flavor of tomatoes, making them tastier and more aromatic. Moreover, basil acts as a natural pest repellent, warding off insects such as mosquitoes and flies that might otherwise harm the tomato plants. This synergistic relationship not only improves the overall health and productivity of the tomatoes but also contributes to a more vibrant and sustainable garden environment. The combined planting of these two enhances both their growth and their resistance to pests, making it a highly beneficial pairing for gardeners.

Chamomile to Improve Seed Germination

Chamomile is highly regarded in the gardening community for its ability to enhance seed germination. This beneficial herb releases chemicals that support the growth and health of neighboring plants. When planted near seed beds or used as a tea to water seeds, chamomile can significantly improve germination rates. Its natural antibacterial and antifungal properties also help protect young seedlings from pathogens that can impede their development. Incorporating chamomile into your garden not only boosts the success rate of sprouting seeds but also fosters a healthier, more resilient start for your garden's new growth.

Chives to Prevent Apple Scab

Planting chives around apple trees can be an effective natural strategy to prevent the fungal disease known as apple scab. Chives emit a strong scent and possess sulfur compounds, which are natural fungicides. These properties help to ward off the fungus that causes scab, protecting the apple trees from the unsightly blemishes and potential fruit loss associated with the disease. Incorporating chives into your orchard not only enhances the overall health of your apple trees but also adds a layer of aesthetic appeal and practical utility, as chives can be harvested for culinary use while they protect your fruit trees.

Corn by Squash for Shade

Planting corn alongside squash is a traditional companion gardening technique that leverages the natural growth habits of both plants for mutual benefit. Corn grows tall and provides a natural shade canopy for the squash, which thrives in slightly cooler temperatures shielded from the intense midday sun. This shade helps reduce the evaporation of moisture from the soil, maintaining a cooler root environment and reducing the stress on squash plants during hot weather. Additionally, the squash's broad leaves act as a living mulch, suppressing weeds and helping to retain soil moisture, which benefits the corn in return. This interplanting not only optimizes space but also creates a symbiotic environment where both plants can thrive.

Dill to Attract Beneficial Insects

Dill is an excellent plant for attracting beneficial insects to the garden, serving as an effective companion plant that enhances overall garden health. Its fragrant foliage and bright yellow flowers are particularly attractive to ladybugs, wasps, and hoverflies, which are natural predators of many common garden pests, including aphids and caterpillars. By planting dill among your vegetables and flowers, you create a natural pest control station that encourages these helpful insects to take up residence. This not only helps control pest populations naturally but also promotes a more balanced ecosystem in your garden, reducing the need for chemical insecticides.

Lemon Balm to Attract Bees

Lemon balm, with its fragrant leaves and profuse blooms, is a magnet for bees in the garden. This perennial herb emits a strong lemony scent, which bees find irresistible, drawing them in to pollinate your plants. The presence of bees buzzing around lemon balm significantly enhances pollination rates, boosting fruit and vegetable yields across your garden. Planting lemon balm not only supports the local bee population but also encourages a thriving, biodiverse garden ecosystem, making it an excellent choice for gardeners looking to increase pollination and enjoy the delightful sight of bees at work.

Nasturtiums to Lure Aphids

Nasturtiums serve a strategic role in the garden by acting as a trap crop for aphids, effectively diverting these pests away from more valuable plants. The vibrant, colorful flowers of nasturtiums are highly attractive to aphids, drawing them in and keeping them occupied. By planting nasturtiums around the perimeter of your garden or near susceptible crops, you can significantly reduce aphid attacks on important plants. This not only protects your vegetables and flowers but also reduces the need for chemical pest control. Using nasturtiums as a natural aphid lure is an environmentally friendly strategy that enhances garden health and maintains the balance of the ecosystem.

Onion and Carrot Pairing

Pairing onions with carrots in the garden is a classic example of companion planting that provides mutual benefits to both crops. Onions help to repel carrot flies, which are attracted to the scent of carrot leaves but are deterred by the strong aroma of onion. Conversely, the scent of carrots can help mask the onions, making them less appealing to onion flies. This natural pest control strategy reduces damage to both crops without the need for chemical pesticides, promoting healthier growth and a more productive garden. Additionally, this pairing efficiently uses garden space and can enhance the overall yield of both vegetables, making it a practical and effective gardening technique.

Radish to Protect Cucumbers

Planting radishes among cucumbers can serve as an effective protective strategy in the garden. Radishes are quick to germinate and grow, making them excellent at repelling various insect pests that commonly target cucumber plants, such as cucumber beetles. The radishes act as a trap crop, luring these pests away from cucumbers due to their rapid leaf production and appealing scent. This method not only helps reduce pest damage to the cucumbers but also can improve the overall health and yield of your cucumber plants. Additionally, because radishes grow quickly and are harvested early, they don't compete significantly with cucumbers for space or nutrients, making them an ideal companion in tightly planned garden spaces.

More Companion Gardening Secrets

Secret	Why It Works	What to Do
Marigolds to Deter Pests	Marigolds release chemicals that repel nematodes, aphids, and other pests.	Plant marigolds around tomatoes, peppers, and other susceptible plants.
Garlic to Deter Pests	Garlic has natural fungicidal and pesticidal properties, deterring aphids, borers, and more.	Plant garlic near roses, raspberries, and fruit trees to keep pests away.
Beans to Fix Nitrogen	Beans convert atmospheric nitrogen into forms usable by plants, enriching the soil.	Plant beans near corn or other nitrogen-loving plants to enhance soil fertility.
Cabbage and Dill	Dill attracts wasps that prey on cabbage pests, improving plant health.	Plant dill near cabbage to naturally control pest populations.
Carrots Love Tomatoes	Tomatoes provide partial shade and root exudates that help deter carrot pests.	Plant carrots underneath or near tomato plants for improved growth and pest control.
Borage to Benefit Strawberries	Borage improves strawberry growth and resilience while deterring pests.	Plant borage next to strawberry plants to boost health and deter pests.
Mint with Cabbage	Mint deters cabbage moths.	Plant mint around cabbage and other brassicas to keep pests away.
Peas with Corn	Peas use corn stalks for support and fix nitrogen.	Plant peas around the base of corn to help both crops thrive.
Spinach under Strawberries	Spinach benefits from the shade provided by strawberry plants.	Plant spinach in the shadow of strawberry plants for better growth.
Calendula with Squash	Calendula attracts pollinators and deters some squash pests.	Plant calendula around squash plants to boost health and pollination.
Cucumbers with Sunflowers	Sunflowers provide a climbing frame and shade for cucumbers.	Plant cucumbers near sunflower stems to use as natural trellises.
Sage with Carrots	Sage repels carrot fly.	Plant sage near carrots to help prevent carrot fly infestations.
Petunias with Beans	Petunias repel bean beetles.	Surround bean plants with petunias to protect against pests.
Oregano with Broccoli	Oregano deters pests that target broccoli.	Plant oregano near broccoli to naturally control pest populations.
Catnip with Eggplant	Catnip repels flea beetles, which are common pests on eggplants.	Plant catnip around eggplant to keep flea beetles at bay.
Lettuce with Tall Flowers	Tall flowers provide shade for lettuce, which prefers cooler temperatures.	Plant lettuce in the shade of taller flowers to keep it cool and moist.
Rosemary with Beans	Rosemary repels bean beetles and improves overall plant health.	Plant rosemary near bean plants to enhance growth and deter pests.
Celery with Leeks	Celery and leeks mutually benefit from each other's pest deterrent properties.	Plant celery and leeks together to naturally deter pests affecting both.
Asparagus with Tomatoes	Tomatoes repel the asparagus beetle.	Plant tomatoes near asparagus to keep asparagus beetles away.

Secret	Why It Works	What to Do
Basil with Peppers	Basil improves the flavor of peppers and repels some pests.	Plant basil near peppers to enhance their flavor and deter pests.
Thyme with Cabbage	Thyme deters cabbage worms.	Plant thyme around cabbage to protect against cabbage worms.
Parsley with Corn	Parsley attracts beneficial insects that prey on corn pests.	Plant parsley near corn to improve pest control.
Lovage with Tomatoes	Lovage improves the health and flavor of tomatoes.	Plant lovage near tomato plants for better growth and flavor.
Tansy with Fruit Trees	Tansy repels flying insects and can improve soil quality.	Plant tansy around the base of fruit trees to deter pests.
Rue with Roses	Rue repels Japanese beetles that commonly attack roses.	Plant rue near rose bushes to help keep beetles away.
Yarrow with Fruit Trees	Yarrow attracts beneficial insects and enhances soil nutrients.	Plant yarrow near fruit trees to attract pollinators and improve soil.

CHAPTER 4: PLANT CARE & MAINTENANCE

Maintaining a thriving garden requires more than just planting seeds and watering; it demands consistent and thoughtful care to ensure each plant reaches its full potential. In this chapter, we delve into a variety of techniques and tips that have been passed down through generations to help you master the art of plant care. From innovative methods like using cinnamon as a natural rooting hormone to traditional practices such as pruning for productivity, these time-tested secrets will provide you with the tools to nurture a flourishing garden. Whether you're dealing with fragile seedlings or mature plants, the strategies outlined here will help you manage every aspect of plant maintenance with confidence and expertise.

Understanding the unique needs of your plants and providing the right care at the right time is crucial for garden success. We'll explore creative uses of common household items, such as using egg cartons for seed starting and pantyhose for gentle plant support, making plant care both cost-effective and sustainable. Additionally, we'll cover essential practices like deep watering techniques to promote strong root systems and using homemade fertilizers to boost plant health. By integrating these diverse approaches into your gardening routine, you'll be well-equipped to address challenges and maximize the health and productivity of your plants, ensuring a vibrant and bountiful garden season after season.

Apple Cider Vinegar for Blossom Boost

Apple cider vinegar (ACV) can be a remarkable aid in the garden, particularly for boosting blossom development in fruit-bearing plants. When diluted properly—typically a small amount of ACV mixed with water—this natural elixir can help lower soil pH slightly, creating a more favorable environment for blossoms to thrive. The mild acidity of ACV serves as a gentle stimulant, encouraging the plants to produce more blossoms, which potentially leads to a higher yield of fruits. This technique is especially beneficial for gardeners looking to enhance the productivity of their fruit trees and shrubs, providing a simple, organic method to promote plant health and increase fruit production.

Aspirin Water Mix

Using an aspirin water mix in your garden is an inventive way to boost plant health and defense mechanisms. Aspirin, containing salicylic acid, mimics a natural hormone in plants that triggers their disease resistance pathways. When dissolved in water—usually at a ratio of one or two aspirin tablets to a gallon of water—and sprayed onto the foliage, this mixture can effectively increase the plant's ability to fend off diseases and stressors. This method is particularly useful for strengthening plants before they are hit by a wave of disease or during periods of unexpected environmental stress, like a sudden cold snap or drought, helping to ensure they remain robust and healthy.

Blossom Thinning

Blossom thinning is a crucial technique used to manage the productivity and health of fruit-bearing plants. By selectively removing a portion of the blossoms or young fruit from a plant, gardeners can prevent overcrowding on branches, which not only reduces the strain on the plant but also improves the size, quality, and uniformity of the fruit produced. This method ensures that the plant's resources are more effectively distributed among the remaining fruits. Blossom thinning is particularly beneficial for fruit trees such as apples, peaches, and pears, where too many fruits developing close together can lead to smaller, less desirable outcomes. By thinning blossoms early in the season, gardeners can directly influence the harvest, increasing the likelihood of a bountiful and healthy yield.

Cinnamon Rooting Hormone

Cinnamon is not only a beloved spice but also an effective natural rooting hormone for gardeners looking to propagate their plants. The compound cinnamaldehyde, found in cinnamon, acts as an antifungal agent that helps prevent cuttings from rotting, thus enhancing the chances of successful root development. To use cinnamon as a rooting hormone, simply dip the fresh cut end of a plant cutting into ground cinnamon powder before planting it in the soil. This method is especially useful for gardeners who prefer organic gardening practices, as it avoids the use of synthetic chemicals. Cinnamon can help ensure that cuttings remain healthy and free from microbial infections as they develop roots, promoting robust growth in new plants.

Club Soda for Rapid Growth

Club soda can be a surprising but effective boost for plant growth due to its mineral content. The beverage contains essential nutrients like potassium, phosphorus, and magnesium, which are vital for healthy plant development. When used to water plants, club soda can expedite growth by providing these nutrients in a readily available form, encouraging more vigorous and robust plant development. To utilize club soda effectively, simply replace regular watering with room temperature club soda occasionally—ideally no more than once a week to avoid any potential negative effects from excess salts. This method can be particularly beneficial for indoor potted plants or gardens that have nutrient-poor soil, helping to supplement their nutritional needs and stimulate faster growth.

Cooking Oil for Plant Shine

Using cooking oil on plants can be an effective way to enhance their aesthetic appeal by giving leaves a polished, shiny appearance. A light coating of a mild oil like vegetable or mineral oil can help dust and debris slide right off the leaves, making the plant look more vibrant and healthy. To apply, mix a small amount of oil with water and a drop of mild soap (to help the oil emulsify and spread evenly) in a spray bottle. Mist the solution lightly onto the leaves of the plant, then gently wipe them with a soft cloth to distribute the oil evenly. This not only cleans and shines the leaves but can also help prevent pests like aphids and mites, which are deterred by the oily layer. However, it's important to use this method sparingly and avoid over-application, as too much oil can clog the pores of the leaves and hinder the plant's ability to breathe.

Deep Watering Techniques

Deep watering techniques are essential for fostering deep, healthy root systems in plants, which enhance stability and drought resistance. This method involves slowly watering the base of plants, allowing the water to seep deeply into the soil, rather than just moistening the surface. Utilizing tools like soaker hoses, drip irrigation systems, or even a low trickle from a garden hose can make this process more efficient. By watering less frequently but more thoroughly, you not only conserve water but also encourage plants to develop strong, extensive root networks. This technique is particularly beneficial for trees and shrubs, as well as vegetable plants, making them more resilient and boosting productivity.

Egg Cartons for Seed Starting

Egg cartons offer a simple and eco-friendly solution for starting seeds. Made from biodegradable materials like paper or cardboard, these cartons provide an ideal, low-cost environment for seed germination. Each compartment can be filled with soil, where seeds can be sown individually. This not only helps in managing the space efficiently but also prevents the roots of young seedlings from becoming entangled, making transplantation easier and less disruptive to the plants. After the seedlings have grown enough to be transplanted, the entire compartment can be cut from the carton and planted directly into the ground. The carton material will naturally decompose in the soil, minimizing transplant shock and supporting sustainable gardening practices. This method is especially useful for gardeners looking to maximize their resources while minimizing waste.

Honey Water to Boost Plant Cuttings

Honey water is a natural and effective way to boost the success of plant cuttings. Honey acts as a rooting hormone due to its natural antibacterial and antifungal properties, which help protect cuttings from pathogens and decay as they develop new roots. To make honey water, simply dissolve one to two tablespoons of honey in two cups of boiled water, allowing it to cool before use. Dip the cut ends of the cuttings into the solution before planting them in the soil. This not only increases the likelihood of the cuttings taking root but also promotes healthier, more vigorous growth. Using honey water is a safe, chemical-free alternative to synthetic rooting hormones, making it a favored choice among organic gardeners.

Pantyhose to Support Plants

Pantyhose can be surprisingly useful in the garden as a gentle yet sturdy support for growing plants. Their soft, flexible material makes them ideal for tying up plants without damaging their stems or restricting growth. This is particularly valuable for supporting heavy flowering plants, climbing vines, or vegetables like tomatoes and cucumbers that can benefit from vertical support. To use pantyhose for plant support, simply cut them into strips and use these strips to tie the plants to stakes, trellises, or cages. The elasticity of the pantyhose allows the plant some movement while holding it securely, which can help prevent breakage from winds or the weight of maturing fruits. Additionally, because pantyhose are breathable and expandable, they can accommodate the growing girth of the plant stems, reducing the risk of cutting into or constricting the plant tissue.

Pruning for Productivity

Pruning is an essential gardening technique that significantly enhances plant productivity by focusing the plant's energy on its most promising parts. Strategic pruning removes dead or overgrown branches and stems, which not only improves the plant's overall health and appearance but also encourages the development of new, vigorous growth. For fruit trees and berry bushes, pruning helps to increase sunlight penetration and air circulation throughout the plant, reducing the risk of disease and promoting better fruit set and size. In the case of flowering plants and vegetables, removing certain parts can stimulate the plant to produce more flowers and fruits, as it redirects its resources from sustaining unnecessary leaves towards reproduction. Proper pruning techniques vary among different plant species and are timed according to their specific growth cycles and fruiting habits to maximize yield and ensure the health of the garden.

Sponges for Humidity Trays

Sponges in humidity trays are a clever and effective way to maintain the necessary moisture levels for plants that thrive in humid environments, such as orchids, ferns, and tropical houseplants. Placing wet sponges in a tray beneath plant pots creates a microclimate that mimics natural humid conditions, promoting healthier growth. This method is particularly beneficial in dry indoor spaces, where heating or air conditioning can reduce air moisture. It's important to keep the sponges moist but not overly saturated to prevent mold and fungal growth. Regular cleaning and refreshing of the sponges ensure that plants benefit from clean, fresh moisture, making this technique both eco-friendly and cost-effective.

Sugar for Root Health

Using sugar in the garden can surprisingly benefit root health by providing an easily accessible energy source for beneficial soil microbes. These microbes, in turn, help in breaking down organic matter and facilitating nutrient absorption by plant roots. To apply sugar for root health, a light sprinkling of granulated sugar around the base of the plants can stimulate microbial activity. However, it's important to use this method sparingly, as excessive sugar can lead to unwanted fungal growth or attract pests.

Generally, a teaspoon of sugar per plant, dissolved in water, and applied once or twice a season is sufficient. This simple and cost-effective treatment can enhance root development and overall plant vitality, promoting a more robust and healthy garden.

Sugar Water for Seedlings

Sugar water can be a beneficial supplement for seedlings, providing them with an extra boost of energy that supports early growth stages. By mimicking the natural process where plants derive energy from photosynthesis, a mild sugar water solution can help young plants develop stronger and faster when their access to natural sunlight is limited, such as in indoor setups or during overcast weather. To prepare, dissolve a small amount of sugar—about a teaspoon per liter of water—and use this solution to water seedlings sparingly. This should be done occasionally, not as a replacement for regular watering, to avoid overstimulation and potential root damage. Properly managed, sugar water can encourage vigorous seedling growth, setting a robust foundation for future plant development.

Tin Cans for Seedling Protection

Tin cans can be effectively repurposed as protective shields for seedlings, safeguarding them from various external threats like harsh winds, heavy rain, and pests. By removing both ends of a clean tin can and placing it around a seedling, you create a sturdy barrier that can shield vulnerable young plants during their critical growth phases. This makeshift cylinder not only protects the seedlings from physical damage but also helps in creating a microclimate that retains moisture and warmth, enhancing growth. It's essential to ensure the can is securely placed in the soil to prevent it from being blown over and to remove it as the plant grows taller and outgrows the enclosure. Using tin cans is a simple, cost-effective method that helps young plants establish themselves in a new environment, promoting healthier development and resilience.

Vodka for Flower Preservation

Vodka can be an unconventional yet effective tool for preserving cut flowers and extending their vase life. The alcohol in vodka acts as an antimicrobial agent, inhibiting the growth of bacteria in the water that can cause flowers to decay prematurely. To use vodka for flower preservation, add just a few drops of vodka (or any clear spirits) to the water in your flower vase along with a teaspoon of sugar. The sugar provides nutrients to the flowers, while the vodka keeps the water clean and free from bacteria. This combination helps keep the stems clear, allowing the flowers to absorb water and nutrients more effectively, thus keeping them fresh and vibrant for a longer period. Change the water every few days, refreshing the vodka and sugar each time to maintain the benefits.

Wool Socks for Plant Frost Cover

Wool socks can serve as an innovative and resourceful method for protecting plants from frost. The natural fibers of wool provide excellent insulation against cold, helping to maintain a warmer temperature around the plant. To use wool socks as a frost cover, simply slip them over the top of smaller plants or seedlings during chilly nights. The socks will help trap heat and prevent the cold air from damaging sensitive plant tissues. This method is particularly useful for sudden cold snaps when plants might not be acclimated to a drop in temperature. Additionally, wool is breathable, allowing moisture to escape and preventing condensation from building up underneath the cover, which could lead to fungal diseases. Removing the socks during the day allows the plants to get sunlight and air, minimizing any risk of overheating or suffocation.

More Plant Care & Maintenance Secrets

Secret	Why It Works	What to Do
Banana Peel Tea	Provides potassium, calcium, and other nutrients to promote healthy plant growth.	Soak banana peels in water for 2-3 days and use the liquid to water plants.
Hydrogen Peroxide for Root Health	Oxygenates the soil and prevents root rot by killing harmful bacteria.	Mix one part hydrogen peroxide with four parts water and apply to the soil around the plant roots.
Blackstrap Molasses	Feeds beneficial soil microbes and provides a rich source of nutrients.	Mix one tablespoon of blackstrap molasses with a gallon of water and use it to water plants.
Cornmeal for Fungus Control	Acts as a natural antifungal agent, suppressing fungal diseases in the soil.	Sprinkle cornmeal around the base of plants and lightly work it into the soil.
Eggshell Mulch	Adds calcium to the soil and deters pests like slugs and snails.	Crush eggshells and spread them around the base of plants.
Green Tea Foliar Spray	Provides antioxidants and nutrients, promoting healthier foliage.	Brew green tea, let it cool, and spray it onto plant leaves.
Aloe Vera Gel for Plant Health	Stimulates growth and boosts the immune system of plants.	Dilute aloe vera gel with water and use it as a foliar spray or soil drench.
Milk Spray for Powdery Mildew	Contains natural antifungal properties that combat powdery mildew.	Mix one part milk with nine parts water and spray onto affected plant leaves.
Willow Water for Rooting	Contains natural rooting hormones that encourage root development.	Soak chopped willow branches in water for a few days and use the water to soak plant cuttings before planting.
Gelatin for Indoor Plants	Provides nitrogen to support leafy growth in houseplants.	Dissolve a packet of unflavored gelatin in water and use it to water indoor plants.
Tea Tree Oil Spray	Acts as a natural insecticide and fungicide, protecting plants from pests and diseases.	Mix a few drops of tea tree oil with water and spray onto plant leaves.
Garlic Water for Pest Control	Repels a wide range of garden pests with its strong odor.	Crush garlic cloves, soak them in water for a day, strain, and spray the liquid onto plants.
Cinnamon for Ant Control	Deters ants from invading garden areas due to its strong scent.	Sprinkle cinnamon around the base of plants or garden beds.
Rice Water for Leaf Shine	Adds nutrients and promotes healthy, shiny foliage.	Use the water from rinsing rice to water plants or wipe down leaves.
Eucalyptus Oil Spray	Acts as a natural insect repellent, keeping pests away from plants.	Mix a few drops of eucalyptus oil with water and spray onto plant leaves.

CHAPTER 5: WATER MANAGEMENT

Effective water management is a cornerstone of sustainable gardening, ensuring that plants receive the precise amount of water needed to thrive without waste. This chapter explores a variety of innovative and practical strategies to optimize water use in your garden. From simple DIY solutions like creating a drip irrigation system from everyday materials to setting up sophisticated rainwater harvesting systems, these techniques will help you make the most of every drop. You'll also learn about ancient methods such as olla pot irrigation and modern approaches like using soil moisture sensors, providing a comprehensive toolkit for maintaining consistent soil moisture and promoting healthy plant growth.

Understanding and implementing efficient water management practices not only conserves a vital resource but also enhances the resilience and productivity of your garden. We'll delve into methods for capturing and utilizing natural rainfall, such as designing rooftop rainwater collection systems and constructing swales to direct rainwater to where it's needed most. Additionally, we'll cover the use of recycled materials and household items, such as converting milk jugs into watering cans and using sponges to maintain soil moisture. By incorporating these techniques, you can create a garden that not only flourishes but also supports environmental sustainability, ensuring a vibrant and bountiful space season after season.

Aloe Vera for Water Retention

Aloe Vera is not only renowned for its medicinal properties but also as a practical solution for enhancing water retention in garden soil. This succulent plant naturally thrives in arid conditions, thanks to its ability to store water within its thick, fleshy leaves. When incorporated into garden soil, Aloe Vera acts as a natural moisture reservoir, releasing water slowly into the surrounding soil. This ability makes it an excellent companion in garden beds, helping to maintain moisture levels and reduce the frequency of watering. Additionally, planting Aloe Vera among other plants can improve overall soil structure and increase its water-holding capacity, making it a valuable addition to both ornamental and functional garden spaces focused on sustainability and water conservation.

Drip Irrigation

DIY drip irrigation is a highly efficient and cost-effective method that delivers water directly to the root zone of plants, minimizing wastage due to evaporation and runoff. To set up your own system, you can utilize common household items such as a hose, some tubing, and a punch tool to create holes at intervals matching your plant placements. Attach the tubing to a water source and control the flow with valves or a timer to ensure a slow, steady drip. For a more budget-friendly option, repurpose old plastic bottles or milk jugs by filling them with water, puncturing small holes in the caps, and placing them near plant bases to release water slowly into the soil. This customized system not only maintains optimal soil moisture for plant health and yield but also reduces both water consumption and garden maintenance effort, making it ideal for gardeners in regions with water scarcity or those interested in conserving resources.

Gray Water System for Gardening

A gray water system for gardening provides an innovative way to reuse household wastewater from sinks, showers, and washing machines, redirecting it to irrigate garden plants. This eco-friendly approach conserves water by utilizing it twice—once for household chores and again for gardening—significantly reducing the overall water consumption. When setting up a gray water system, it's essential to use only biodegradable soaps and detergents to avoid harming plants with harmful chemicals. Additionally, a simple filtration system should be incorporated to remove solid particles and prevent clogging. Properly designed, a gray water system not only ensures that garden plants receive adequate moisture but also promotes sustainable water management practices, making it a practical solution for environmentally conscious gardeners looking to maximize their water efficiency.

Milk Jug Watering Can

Creating a watering can from an old milk jug is a simple and effective way to recycle household items into useful gardening tools. By piercing small holes in the lid of a clean milk jug, you can craft a makeshift watering can that provides a gentle shower of water, ideal for young seedlings and delicate plants. This DIY solution not only reduces waste but also allows for precise water control, helping to avoid overwatering and minimizing soil disturbance. The handle on the milk jug makes it easy to carry and pour, offering convenience and functionality. This economical and eco-friendly approach to garden watering is particularly beneficial for gardeners looking to equip themselves on a budget while practicing sustainability.

Olla Pot Irrigation

Olla pot irrigation is an ancient and efficient watering technique that uses unglazed clay pots buried in the garden to slowly release water directly to plant roots. This method minimizes water waste and evaporation by delivering moisture underground, right where plants need it most. To implement, gardeners fill the olla pots with water, which then gradually seeps through the porous clay walls and into the soil, providing a consistent and controlled supply of water. This targeted irrigation promotes deeper root growth and reduces the need for frequent watering, making it especially useful in dry climates or during hot weather. Olla pot irrigation not only conserves water but also enhances plant health and growth by maintaining optimal soil moisture levels.

Rain Barrel Setup for Rainwater Harvesting

Installing rain barrels is a practical and environmentally friendly way to collect and reuse rainwater for gardening, significantly reducing reliance on municipal water supplies and lowering water bills. By positioning barrels under downspouts, gardeners can capture rainwater runoff from roofs, which can then be stored and used during dry periods. This method of water conservation not only helps in maintaining a lush garden during water restrictions but also reduces the impact on local water resources. Additionally, rainwater is often softer than tap water, lacking in salts and chemicals, which makes it better for watering plants that may be sensitive to the additives in municipal water supplies. Setting up rain barrels is a straightforward step towards sustainable gardening, helping to save water and decrease utility expenses.

Rain Gauge for Watering Decisions

Using a rain gauge in your garden is a simple yet effective way to make informed watering decisions. By measuring the amount of rainfall received, gardeners can adjust their watering schedules based on actual needs rather than guessing. This ensures that plants receive the right amount of water—neither too much nor too little—contributing to healthier growth and development. A rain gauge helps prevent overwatering, which can lead to root rot and other water-related plant diseases, and under-watering, which can stress plants and reduce their productivity. Integrating a rain gauge into your gardening routine allows for more precise water management, optimizing your watering practices to suit the specific conditions of your garden and the current weather patterns.

Rooftop Rainwater Collection

Rooftop rainwater collection is an efficient and sustainable method to harness natural rainfall for garden and household use. This system involves diverting rainwater from your roof into storage containers or barrels via gutters and downspouts. The collected water can then be used to irrigate gardens, wash cars, or even, with proper treatment, for household purposes. Implementing a rooftop rainwater collection system reduces dependence on municipal water systems, conserves resources, and can significantly lower water bills. Additionally, using rainwater for irrigation is beneficial for plants as it is free from the chlorine and other chemicals typically found in tap water. Setting up a rooftop collection system is a proactive step towards sustainable living, providing a plentiful and eco-friendly water supply for various needs.

Soda Bottle Drip Irrigation

Soda bottle drip irrigation is an innovative and resourceful method for watering plants efficiently, particularly useful in areas where water conservation is essential. This DIY system involves using empty soda bottles as individual drip irrigators. Simply puncture small holes in the cap of a cleaned soda bottle, fill it with water, and invert it into the soil near the plant. The water slowly drips directly to the plant's root zone, providing a steady, controlled supply of moisture. This method minimizes water wastage due to evaporation and runoff, ensuring that water is delivered where it's most needed. Soda bottle drip irrigation is not only economical but also an excellent way to repurpose plastic bottles, reducing waste and promoting sustainability in gardening practices.

Soil Moisture Sensors

Soil moisture sensors are a valuable tool for optimizing irrigation practices in gardening and agriculture. These devices measure the moisture content in the soil, providing real-time data that can help gardeners make informed decisions about when and how much to water their plants. By using soil moisture sensors, you can prevent both overwatering and underwatering, ensuring that plants receive the precise amount of water they need for optimal growth. This targeted watering approach not only conserves water but also promotes healthier plant development by maintaining ideal soil moisture levels. Installing soil moisture sensors in a garden or farm can lead to more efficient water use, better crop yields, and a reduction in water-related plant stress.

Sponge as Moisture Keeper

Using a sponge as a moisture keeper in plant pots is a clever and effective way to maintain consistent soil moisture, especially beneficial for container gardening. Sponges are highly absorbent, capable of holding several times their weight in water, and gradually release it back into the soil as it begins to dry, ensuring a steady supply of moisture. To utilize this method, place a clean, new sponge at the bottom of the pot before adding soil and planting. The sponge will absorb excess water during watering and then slowly release it back, keeping the soil evenly moist and promoting healthier root growth and plant vitality. This technique is particularly useful during hot weather or in dry indoor environments where soil moisture quickly evaporates.

Swale Creation for Rain Capture

Creating a swale is an effective landscaping technique used to capture and redirect rainwater, optimizing moisture distribution and reducing runoff. A swale is essentially a shallow trench built along the contour of the land, often filled with absorbent material like gravel and lined with permeable soil and vegetation. This design allows the swale to intercept rainwater runoff, holding it long enough to gradually percolate into the ground, replenishing groundwater and irrigating plants naturally. By strategically placing swales in areas of your garden or property where water typically accumulates or flows, you can harness this natural resource, enhancing plant growth and reducing the need for supplemental watering. Additionally, swales can help prevent erosion and flooding, making them a practical and environmentally friendly addition to landscape design, especially in regions prone to heavy rains.

Terracotta Water Spikes

Terracotta water spikes are a practical and aesthetically pleasing solution for consistent soil moisture, ideal for busy gardeners or those in hot climates. Made from porous terracotta clay, these spikes are designed to slowly release water directly to plant roots when attached to an inverted water-filled bottle. The terracotta's porous nature allows for a gradual seepage of water, ensuring plants receive a steady, controlled supply of moisture without the risk of overwatering. This method is particularly useful for maintaining plant health during extended periods of heat or absence, ensuring optimal hydration for healthier growth while seamlessly blending into the garden environment.

Tuna Can for Irrigation Gauge

Using a tuna can as an irrigation gauge is a simple, effective method for ensuring your lawn or garden receives the right amount of water. Place an empty tuna can in the area being watered and run your sprinkler system or hose until the can collects about one inch of water, which is typically the recommended amount per watering session to maintain healthy plant and lawn growth. This straightforward technique helps gardeners and homeowners avoid over or under-watering, promoting water efficiency and healthier plant growth. It also serves as a practical tool for adjusting and calibrating irrigation systems to ensure even water distribution throughout the garden or lawn.

Wicking Bed System

A wicking bed system is an innovative and water-efficient gardening solution, particularly effective in areas prone to drought. This system utilizes a water reservoir built beneath the soil surface, which allows water to "wick" upwards through the soil by capillary action directly to the plant roots. This method ensures that water is delivered where it's needed most, reducing evaporation and water wastage. Wicking beds are especially useful for vegetable gardening, as they provide consistent moisture, crucial for steady growth and yield. Additionally, because the water is contained below, there's less weed growth and no water runoff, making it a highly sustainable option. Installing a wicking bed can save considerable water over traditional top-watering methods and is an excellent choice for environmentally conscious gardeners looking to maximize efficiency and productivity in their gardens.

More Water Management Secrets

Secret	Why It Works	What to Do
Crushed Gravel for Soil Drainage	Enhances soil drainage and prevents waterlogging.	Mix crushed gravel into garden soil to improve its structure and drainage capacity.
Plastic Bottle Reservoirs	Provides a slow release of water directly to plant roots.	Cut the bottom off a plastic bottle, bury it neck down near plant roots, and fill with water.
Drip Line Tuning	Optimizes water usage and ensures even distribution.	Regularly check and adjust drip irrigation lines to ensure they are delivering water evenly and efficiently.
Mulching with Grass Clippings	Retains soil moisture and adds nutrients as it decomposes.	Spread a layer of grass clippings around plants to help conserve moisture and suppress weeds.
Perlite for Soil Aeration	Improves soil aeration and water retention.	Mix perlite into potting soil to enhance drainage and prevent soil compaction.

CHAPTER 6: WEED PREVENTION AND REMOVAL

Effective weed management is a cornerstone of successful gardening, ensuring that your plants thrive without competition for nutrients, light, and space. Weeds not only mar the beauty of a garden but also harbor pests and diseases, making their control crucial. This section explores a variety of innovative and traditional methods for both preventing and removing weeds, utilizing everything from household items to specific gardening products. Techniques such as using boiling water, vinegar, or salt solutions exploit natural, readily available resources to tackle weeds directly, offering eco-friendly alternatives to chemical herbicides. Other methods, like laying down cardboard or newspaper, provide a physical barrier to suppress weed growth and decay into the soil, enhancing its structure and fertility.

Additionally, integrating living solutions such as clover as living mulch or using corn gluten as a pre-emergent weed preventer harnesses nature's own mechanisms for maintaining balance and health in the garden. Strategies like flame weeding and applying mulch layers effectively manage weed issues while also contributing to the garden's ecological well-being by improving soil health and reducing the need for frequent maintenance. These diverse approaches offer gardeners a toolbox of options to maintain pristine and productive gardens by curbing the growth of unwanted plants in a sustainable and often cost-effective manner.

Vodka to Kill Weeds

Vodka can be an effective natural herbicide for controlling weeds in your garden. The alcohol in vodka works by stripping away the waxy cuticle that covers the leaves of the weed, causing them to dehydrate and die. To use vodka as a weed killer, mix one ounce of vodka with a couple of cups of water and a few drops of dish soap to enhance the mixture's ability to cling to the leaves. Apply this solution directly to the leaves of the weeds, preferably during the sunniest part of the day, as sunlight accelerates the effects of the alcohol. This method is particularly effective for weeds situated in direct sunlight and should be used cautiously to avoid harming nearby desired plants.

Baking Soda Weed Killer

Baking soda is a handy and eco-friendly option for tackling weeds, especially in cracks on driveways, walkways, or between patio stones. The sodium content in baking soda acts as a desiccant, drying out weeds upon contact. To use baking soda as a weed killer, simply sprinkle a generous amount directly onto the weed, especially focusing on the foliage and at the base where the stem meets the soil. The application is most effective when done on a dry, sunny day to ensure the baking soda stays in place and maximizes its drying effect. This method is safe for use around pets and children and adds to the soil's alkalinity, which can help prevent future weed growth in areas where high soil pH is tolerated.

Boiling Water Weed Killer

Boiling water is an extremely effective and environmentally friendly method for killing weeds, offering a quick and chemical-free option. Simply pouring boiling water directly onto the weeds causes immediate damage to the plant's cell structure, effectively killing them from the roots upwards. This method is particularly useful for weeds growing in cracks in pavements or driveways, and other hard-to-reach areas where selective application won't harm nearby desired plants. Since boiling water does not leave any residual chemicals, it is safe for use in gardens where vegetables or fruits are grown, ensuring that the surrounding soil and plants remain uncontaminated. However, care should be taken to precisely target the weeds to avoid damaging nearby plants that you want to keep.

Cardboard as Path Weed Blocker

Using cardboard as a weed blocker along garden paths is a highly effective, sustainable method for controlling unwanted growth. Cardboard acts as a physical barrier, blocking light and suppressing weed germination and growth beneath it. To use, simply lay flat sheets of cardboard directly over the areas where you want to prevent weeds. Overlap the edges to ensure there are no gaps for weeds to push through. Once in place, the cardboard can be covered with mulch or gravel to improve aesthetics and help hold it down. Over time, the cardboard will naturally decompose, enriching the soil with organic matter while continuing to suppress weeds. This method is particularly appealing for organic gardeners looking to avoid chemical treatments and reduce waste by repurposing used cardboard.

Clover as Living Mulch

Clover serves as an excellent living mulch, offering multiple benefits for garden health and weed suppression. Planting clover among or around other crops helps to cover bare soil, which naturally reduces the growth of weeds by blocking sunlight and competing for resources. Additionally, clover is a legume, which means it has the ability to fix nitrogen from the air into the soil, enhancing soil fertility and reducing the need for synthetic fertilizers. The dense mat of clover also helps to retain soil moisture and prevent erosion, while its flowers attract beneficial insects like bees, which are essential for pollination. This makes clover not only an effective tool for managing weeds but also a contributor to a more biodiverse and sustainable garden ecosystem.

Corn Gluten Weed Preventer

Corn gluten meal acts as a natural pre-emergent weed preventer, providing an organic solution to garden weed control. This by-product of the corn milling process contains proteins that inhibit root formation in seedlings shortly after they germinate. When applied to the soil, corn gluten meal effectively reduces the number of new weeds by preventing these young weeds from establishing their root systems, though it won't kill existing weeds. For best results, apply corn gluten meal to areas of your garden where weeds are a recurring problem, before the growing season begins, and when the soil is dry. Besides its weed-suppressing properties, corn gluten meal also adds nitrogen to the soil, serving as a natural fertilizer that promotes the growth of desired plants.

Cornmeal as a Pre-emergent

Cornmeal, specifically corn gluten meal, is a natural and effective pre-emergent weed control option that gardeners can use to prevent weed seeds from germinating. When applied to the soil, cornmeal acts as an organic herbicide by inhibiting root development in weed seedlings. This disruption occurs just as the seeds begin to sprout, which prevents them from establishing a robust root system, effectively reducing weed emergence. To utilize cornmeal as a pre-emergent, it should be evenly spread over the garden soil early in the spring before weeds begin to grow, and the soil should be slightly moistened afterwards to activate its properties. Additionally, cornmeal also enriches the soil with nitrogen, benefiting the overall soil health and aiding the growth of garden plants. It's important to note that while cornmeal can deter new weeds, it does not affect existing weeds and should be part of a broader integrated weed management strategy.

Flame Weeding

Flame weeding is an effective method for controlling weeds using a burst of intense heat to kill unwanted plants. This technique involves the use of a propane torch to deliver a quick, direct flame to the weeds, causing the plant cells to burst and the weeds to wilt and die. Flame weeding is especially useful for treating weeds in hard-to-reach places, such as cracks in driveways or walkways, and around garden perimeters where precision is necessary to avoid damaging desired plants. It's an environmentally friendly alternative to chemical herbicides, as it leaves no harmful residues and only targets the plants it is applied to. However, it requires careful handling to ensure safety and effectiveness, ideally performed during cooler, moist conditions to reduce the risk of unintended fires. This method is best suited for young, annual weeds and can be a part of an integrated weed management approach in any garden.

Landscape Fabric Barrier

Landscape fabric barrier is a popular method for weed control, particularly effective in maintaining clear areas around ornamental plants, paths, and between garden beds. This permeable fabric is laid over the soil surface to block weed growth by preventing sunlight from reaching the weeds, thus stifying their development. The fabric is breathable, allowing water and nutrients to pass through to the soil beneath, ensuring that desired plants can thrive. To install, the area should be cleared of existing weeds, the fabric laid down, and then secured with garden staples. Mulch is often spread over the top to enhance the aesthetic and help hold the fabric in place. Landscape fabric is especially useful in reducing maintenance time and keeping garden and landscape areas neat and tidy over the long term, although it may require occasional checks to repair tears or gaps where weeds might penetrate.

Lemon Juice as a Natural Herbicide

Lemon juice is a natural herbicide that can effectively manage weed growth in gardens without the use of harsh chemicals. The high acidity of lemon juice works to desiccate weeds upon contact, essentially drying them out and causing them to wither away. To use lemon juice as a weed killer, it can be applied directly to the leaves of the weeds, preferably on a hot, sunny day to enhance its effectiveness. This method is particularly useful for spot treatment in gardens, walkways, or patios where selective weed control is necessary. Mixing lemon juice with vinegar can increase its potency, creating a more effective natural herbicide solution. While eco-friendly and easy to apply, it's important to apply lemon juice carefully to avoid contact with desired plants, as its acidic nature can potentially harm them as well.

Mint Weed Repellent

Mint is renowned not only for its aromatic leaves but also for its aggressive growth, which can be harnessed as a natural weed repellent in the garden. Planting mint strategically can help suppress other less vigorous plants, including weeds, by outcompeting them for space and resources. Mint spreads quickly through its underground runners and can cover bare spots where weeds might otherwise establish. However, because mint can become invasive, it's often best to plant it in contained areas or raised beds where it can't spread uncontrollably. Additionally, the strong scent of mint is disliked by many pests and can deter them from nearby plants. Using mint as a living mulch provides a dual benefit of weed suppression and pest deterrence, making it a useful companion in the garden.

Mulch Overlapping

Overlapping mulch is a highly effective technique for suppressing weeds and maintaining soil health in gardens. By applying a generous layer of organic mulch, such as wood chips, straw, or leaf litter, and ensuring that each layer slightly overlaps the next, gardeners can create a dense barrier that blocks sunlight from reaching the soil surface. This lack of light inhibits weed seed germination and growth, significantly reducing the presence of unwanted plants. Additionally, overlapping mulch helps to retain soil moisture by reducing evaporation, maintains a more consistent soil temperature, and gradually breaks down to add organic matter back into the soil. This not only improves soil structure and fertility but also promotes healthier plant growth. Employing this mulching strategy ensures a tidier garden appearance and reduces the need for frequent weeding and watering.

Newspaper as Biodegradable Blocker

Using newspaper as a biodegradable weed blocker is an environmentally friendly and cost-effective method for managing garden weeds. Layers of newspaper can be laid directly on the soil surface in garden beds, acting as a natural barrier that blocks light and prevents weed seeds from germinating. To use, simply wet the newspaper sheets to keep them in place and then cover them with a layer of organic mulch, such as straw or bark. This not only secures the newspaper but also enhances the aesthetic of the garden. Over time, the newspaper will naturally decompose and enrich the soil with carbon, aiding soil structure and fertility. This method is particularly appealing for organic gardeners looking to suppress weeds without the use of chemical herbicides, while simultaneously recycling household waste and improving soil health.

Rubbing Alcohol Spray

Rubbing alcohol spray is an effective and quick-acting method for controlling weeds in the garden. When diluted with water and sprayed directly onto weed leaves, the alcohol breaks down the waxy cuticle that protects the plant tissues, causing them to dehydrate and die. To create an effective weed-killing solution, mix one part rubbing alcohol with two parts water and transfer it to a spray bottle. This solution should be applied directly to the weeds, ideally during warm, sunny weather to enhance the dehydration process. Care must be taken to target only the weeds, as the solution can also harm desirable plants if contacted. This method is especially useful for spot treatments in paths, driveways, or between garden rows where precision is necessary to avoid damaging nearby plants.

Salt and Vinegar Solution

A salt and vinegar solution is a potent homemade herbicide that can effectively kill weeds. To create this solution, mix one gallon of white vinegar with one cup of salt and a tablespoon of liquid dish soap, which helps the solution adhere to the weed leaves. The acidity of the vinegar and the desiccating properties of the salt work together to quickly dry out and kill the weeds. This mixture should be applied directly to the weeds, ensuring thorough coverage, especially during a sunny day to enhance the effects. It's important to use this solution cautiously, as it can harm soil health and nearby plants. The salt and vinegar solution is best used for controlling weeds in areas where soil health is not a concern, such as cracks in driveways, walkways, and other hard surfaces.

Salt as a Pathway Weed Killer

Using salt as a pathway weed killer is an effective method for managing weeds in non-plant areas such as gravel paths, patios, or driveways. Salt works by dehydrating plants and disrupting the internal water balance of weed cells, causing them to die. To apply, simply sprinkle a small amount of table salt directly onto the weeds, or dissolve the salt in water to create a more controlled, liquid application. Be mindful to apply the salt strictly to the areas where no vegetation is desired, as it can severely affect soil fertility and may inadvertently harm nearby desirable plants or contaminate the soil. This method is especially useful for areas where you want to prevent all plant growth, as the residual saltiness in the soil will inhibit future weed germination and growth.

Salt Spray for Weed Control

Salt spray is a simple and effective method for controlling weeds, particularly useful for areas where plant growth is not wanted, like the cracks in sidewalks and driveways. To create a salt spray, dissolve about one part salt in eight parts hot water, adding a small squirt of dish soap to help the mixture adhere to the weed leaves. Once the salt is fully dissolved, transfer the solution to a spray bottle. When applying, direct the spray onto the weed foliage and the base of the plants to ensure effective uptake. The salt in the solution will cause the weeds to dehydrate and die quickly. However, care should be taken to target only the weeds, as salt can be detrimental to soil health and non-target plants, potentially causing damage if misapplied. This method is best reserved for use in contained areas where you want to prevent any vegetation from growing.

Sawdust Paths to Control Weeds

Using sawdust to cover paths in your garden is an effective and natural method for controlling weed growth. Sawdust acts as a mulch, creating a barrier that suppresses weeds by blocking sunlight and reducing the soil temperature. When applied thickly along garden paths or between rows of plants, sawdust can significantly inhibit the germination and growth of weeds. Additionally, as sawdust decomposes, it adds organic material to the soil, although it can temporarily draw nitrogen away from the soil as it breaks down. To mitigate this, it's advisable to add a nitrogen-rich supplement to areas where sawdust is used extensively. This method not only helps maintain clean and attractive garden paths but also contributes to soil health over time, making it a sustainable choice for organic gardening.

Sugar Weed Suppression

Sugar can be used as an unconventional but effective method for suppressing weed growth in gardens. By sprinkling granulated sugar directly onto the soil around plants, you can inhibit weed growth. The sugar increases the osmotic pressure in the soil, making it harder for weed seeds to draw water. Additionally, sugar can enhance the growth of beneficial bacteria and fungi in the soil, which compete with weeds for resources and space. However, it's important to use this method judiciously, as excessive sugar can also alter soil composition and potentially harm plant roots. Applying a moderate amount of sugar in specific areas where weed growth is a problem can help manage weeds without the use of harsh chemicals, maintaining a more natural garden environment.

Vinegar Weed Killer

Vinegar is a popular and effective organic weed killer, due to its high acetic acid content which can effectively kill young, tender weeds. To use vinegar as a weed killer, simply fill a spray bottle with white vinegar or a stronger horticultural vinegar for more stubborn weeds, and spray it directly onto the leaves and stems of unwanted plants. The acetic acid in the vinegar works by drawing moisture out of the weeds, causing them to dehydrate and die quickly. It is most effective when applied during sunny, dry weather to ensure that the vinegar does not dilute with rainwater and that it maximizes its drying effect. While vinegar is non-selective and can harm any plant it touches, careful application can make it a useful tool for managing weeds in paths, driveways, or other non-crop areas. Avoid spraying it near desirable plants as it can potentially damage or kill them.

More Weed Prevention & Removal Secrets

Secret	Why It Works	What to Do
Vinegar and Soap Solution	The acidity of vinegar combined with the surfactant properties of soap dries out and kills weeds effectively.	Mix one gallon of white vinegar with one tablespoon of liquid dish soap. Spray directly onto weeds on a sunny day for best results.
Epsom Salt Herbicide	Epsom salt dehydrates weeds, killing them while providing magnesium to the soil.	Mix one cup of Epsom salt with two gallons of water and a tablespoon of dish soap. Spray directly on weeds.
Boron for Weed Suppression	Boron is toxic to plants in high quantities, making it effective for controlling weeds.	Dissolve 10 ounces of borax in 2.5 gallons of water and spray on weeds, being careful to avoid desirable plants.
Alfalfa Mulch	Alfalfa contains natural growth inhibitors that prevent weed germination.	Spread a layer of alfalfa mulch around plants to suppress weed growth and enrich the soil.
Copper Wire Rings	Copper repels slugs and snails, preventing them from eating young plants.	Place copper wire rings around the base of plants to create a barrier that slugs and snails avoid.
Plastic Sheeting	Blocks sunlight and prevents weed seed germination.	Cover garden beds with black plastic sheeting before planting to kill existing weeds and prevent new ones.
Ground Clove as Pre-emergent	Contains natural compounds that inhibit weed seed germination.	Sprinkle ground clove around garden beds to prevent weed seeds from sprouting.
Cocoa Hull Mulch	Acts as a natural weed suppressant while adding nutrients to the soil.	Spread a layer of cocoa hull mulch around plants to suppress weeds and improve soil quality.
Soybean Meal	Acts as a pre-emergent herbicide that inhibits weed growth.	Apply soybean meal to garden beds to prevent weed seeds from germinating.
Iron-Based Herbicides	Targets broadleaf weeds without harming grass.	Apply iron-based herbicide products according to package instructions to selectively kill broadleaf weeds.
Peanut Shell Mulch	Provides a natural barrier to weed growth while enriching the soil.	Spread a layer of peanut shell mulch around plants to suppress weeds and improve soil health.
Baking Soda for Driveways	Sodium bicarbonate dehydrates weeds growing in cracks.	Sprinkle baking soda directly onto weeds growing in driveways and sidewalks to kill them.
Overseeding Lawn	Thickening the grass can crowd out weeds.	Regularly overseed your lawn to maintain dense grass that prevents weeds from establishing.
Vinegar and Lemon Juice	A powerful combination that dries out weeds quickly.	Mix equal parts vinegar and lemon juice and spray directly onto weeds during sunny days.
Clove Oil Herbicide	Contains eugenol, which is effective in killing weeds.	Mix clove oil with water and a few drops of dish soap and spray onto weeds.

CHAPTER 7: PEST CONTROL

Effective pest control is essential for maintaining a healthy and productive garden. Pests, ranging from insects to larger animals, can cause significant damage to plants, reducing yields and affecting the overall vitality of a garden. This section explores a variety of innovative and traditional methods for pest management, using household items and natural ingredients to create barriers, traps, and repellents. Techniques such as using beer as a slug trap, aluminum foil to scare birds, and cayenne pepper to deter rabbits offer gardeners environmentally friendly alternatives to chemical pesticides. These methods not only aim to control unwanted pests but also strive to maintain ecological balance, ensuring that beneficial organisms remain unharmed.

In addition to physical and chemical deterrents, strategic planting plays a crucial role in natural pest control. Companion planting, for example, utilizes specific plants like marigolds to repel insect pests naturally, integrating pest management directly into garden design. Other approaches, such as creating garlic barriers or using soap sprays, target specific pests with minimal impact on the garden ecosystem. Each technique highlighted in this section offers practical solutions for gardeners seeking to protect their plants from pests while adhering to sustainable gardening practices. By employing these methods, gardeners can reduce their reliance on synthetic chemicals and foster a more natural, resilient garden environment.

Aluminum Foil Deterrent

Aluminum foil is a versatile and effective tool for deterring various garden pests, including birds, rodents, and insects. By reflecting light and creating a rustling sound when disturbed, aluminum foil can startle and discourage pests from settling in garden areas. Gardeners often use strips of foil around fruit trees or vegetable beds, or even wrap it around the bases of plants. The shiny, moving foil acts as a visual and auditory deterrent, making the environment uncomfortable for pests that are sensitive to light and noise. Additionally, the reflective surface of the aluminum can disorient insects and birds, preventing them from landing and feeding on the plants. This method is not only simple and cost-effective but also environmentally friendly, providing a chemical-free option for protecting your garden's bounty.

Beer Slug Trap

Using beer to trap slugs is an effective and natural method to protect your garden from these common pests. Slugs are attracted to the yeast found in beer, making it an excellent bait. To set up a beer slug trap, simply bury a shallow container, like a cup or a bowl, so that the rim is level with the ground and fill it with cheap beer. The slugs, drawn by the scent, will crawl into the container and drown. Place the traps near affected areas, especially around vegetables and flowers that are prone to slug damage. This method not only helps reduce the slug population in your garden but does so without the use of harmful chemicals, making it safe for the environment and other wildlife. Regularly emptying and refilling the traps will maintain their effectiveness throughout the slug season.

Borax for Ant Control

Borax is a highly effective substance for controlling ant populations in the garden and around the home. When mixed with sweet bait like sugar, Borax acts as a slow-acting poison that ants carry back to their colony, ultimately eliminating the entire nest. To create an ant control solution, mix equal parts Borax and sugar with just enough water to get a syrupy consistency. Place this mixture near ant trails or where you've seen ant activity. The sugar attracts the ants while the Borax poisons them. It's important to use this method cautiously, especially around pets and children, as Borax is toxic when ingested. By strategically placing the bait in targeted areas, you can significantly reduce ant infestations without resorting to harsh chemical pesticides

Cayenne Pepper to Deter Rabbits

Cayenne pepper is an effective natural repellent for deterring rabbits from garden plants. The strong, spicy scent and taste of cayenne pepper make it unappealing to rabbits, who are generally sensitive to strong flavors and odors. To use cayenne pepper as a deterrent, sprinkle the powder directly around the base of plants that are frequently nibbled on by rabbits, or mix it with water to create a spray solution. When applying the spray, cover the plant leaves lightly. This creates an unpleasant environment for rabbits without harming the plants or the environment. Reapplication is necessary, especially after rainfall or regular watering, to maintain its effectiveness. Using cayenne pepper not only helps protect your garden from rabbit damage but does so in a humane and environmentally friendly way.

Chalk Ant Barrier

Chalk is an effective method for creating a natural barrier against ants. The calcium carbonate in the chalk acts as a deterrent, which ants avoid crossing. By drawing thick lines of chalk at entry points such as doorways, windowsills, or around garden areas where ant activity is noticed, you can prevent their access. This method is safe, non-toxic, and easy to apply, although it may require frequent reapplication, especially after exposure to moisture.

Citrus Peel Deterrent

Citrus peels are a natural and aromatic deterrent for various pests, particularly cats and insects. The strong scent of citrus oils found in the peels is unappealing to pests. Scatter fresh or dried citrus peels around garden beds or areas where pests are frequent, or use them to create a natural repellent spray by steeping the peels in hot water. This method is environmentally friendly and adds a pleasant fragrance to your garden or home.

Companion Planting with Marigolds

Marigolds are highly regarded in companion planting for their ability to deter pests, including nematodes and various insects, through the release of natural chemicals from their roots and foliage. Planting marigolds among vegetables and flowers can help protect your garden from pests while also adding vibrant color and beauty. The strong scent of marigolds is especially effective against aphids and mosquitoes, making them an excellent choice for organic pest control strategies.

Cucumber Peels to Deter Ants

Cucumber peels contain compounds that naturally repel ants, making them an excellent choice for an eco-friendly ant deterrent. Placing cucumber peels at entry points, such as window sills or doorways, or directly onto ant trails, can disrupt their activity and drive them away from these areas. The bitterness of the peels is particularly effective against ants, who find the scent and taste unappealing. For best results, replace the peels frequently to maintain their effectiveness, especially in areas of high ant concentration.

Cucumber Slices to Deter Beetles

Cucumber slices can be an effective natural remedy to deter beetles and other garden pests. The cucurbitacin compounds in cucumber are unattractive to many beetle species. Placing fresh slices around the garden, particularly near plants frequently attacked by beetles, can help keep these pests at bay. This method is safe for the garden and non-toxic, offering a simple and sustainable option for protecting your plants without resorting to harsh chemical pesticides.

Eggshell Pest Deterrent

Crushed eggshells act as a natural pest deterrent in gardens, particularly against slugs and snails. The sharp edges of the crushed shells create a physical barrier that is uncomfortable for these pests to cross. Scatter the crushed eggshells around the base of plants vulnerable to slug and snail damage, such as leafy greens and flowers. In addition to deterring pests, eggshells also enrich the soil with calcium as they decompose, contributing to the nutrient content of the garden.

Garlic Barrier for Pests

Garlic is an effective natural repellent against a wide range of pests, including insects and small mammals. Planting garlic around the perimeter of a garden or interspersing it among different crops can create a protective barrier that many pests find offensive. The strong scent of garlic masks the smells of other plants, making it harder for pests to locate their preferred hosts. Additionally, garlic can be made into a spray by steeping crushed cloves in water, which can then be applied directly to plants to enhance pest deterrent effects further.

Garlic Spray for Pests and Fungi

Garlic spray serves as a potent natural deterrent for both pests and fungal diseases. To make garlic spray, blend a few cloves of garlic with water and let the mixture sit overnight. Strain and dilute it with more water before spraying it directly onto the plants. The strong odor of garlic repels a wide array of pests, including aphids, beetles, and caterpillars, while its antifungal properties help prevent outbreaks of powdery mildew and other fungal infections. This spray is particularly useful in organic gardening as it avoids the use of synthetic chemicals, maintaining a healthy and sustainable environment.

Hair as Deer Repellent

Human hair is an effective deer repellent, capitalizing on deer's aversion to human scent. Gather clumps of hair from hairbrushes or local barbershops and place them in mesh bags or directly scatter them around the perimeter of gardens or near specific plants that deer frequently target. The scent of human hair makes deer uneasy and deters them from entering the area. This method is humane, non-toxic, and doubles as a way to recycle hair, making it a practical solution for gardeners in deer-prone areas.

Herb Border for Pest Repellent

Planting a border of aromatic herbs around a garden can naturally repel pests while enhancing the garden's aesthetics and biodiversity. Herbs such as basil, lavender, rosemary, and thyme emit strong scents that are unappealing to many pests, effectively masking the odors of more attractive host plants. This fragrant barrier not only keeps pests at bay but also attracts beneficial insects which aid in pollination and pest control. Furthermore, herb borders can be harvested for culinary and medicinal uses, offering multiple benefits from a single planting strategy.

Lavender Cotton to Deter Moths

Lavender cotton, a low-growing evergreen shrub with gray-green foliage and a strong, pungent smell, is excellent for deterring moths and other insects. The plant's aromatic oils are particularly distasteful to moths, making it an ideal choice for planting in wardrobes, drawers, or around the garden where moth-sensitive plants are grown. Not only does it keep moths away, but lavender cotton also adds a decorative touch to garden spaces and can be used in dried floral arrangements, providing lasting fragrance and pest repellent properties indoors.

Lemon Juice Ant Repellent

Lemon juice is an effective natural repellent against ants due to its strong acidic property, which disrupts their scent trails. By squeezing fresh lemon juice directly along ant entry points or trails, or wiping surfaces with a lemon juice solution, you can create a barrier that ants avoid. The potent citrus scent masks their pheromone trails, making it difficult for them to navigate or communicate. For continued effectiveness, reapply the lemon juice regularly, especially after cleaning or rain, to maintain a protective barrier against these persistent invaders.

Old Jeans for Scarecrows

Old jeans are ideal for crafting scarecrows, a timeless and effective method for deterring birds and other pests from gardens. To create a scarecrow, stuff a pair of old jeans with straw, leaves, or other materials to give it shape, and pair it with a shirt and a hat. Position your scarecrow in the garden where pests are a problem, ensuring it is visible and mobile enough to sway in the wind, which enhances its effectiveness. Scarecrows not only protect crops by scaring away birds and small animals but also add a whimsical element to garden decor.

Pepper Spray for Pests

Pepper spray is a potent homemade pesticide that deters a wide range of garden pests, including insects and small mammals, thanks to the capsaicin found in peppers. To make pepper spray, blend hot peppers with water and a small amount of dish soap, which helps the mixture adhere to plant leaves. Strain the mixture and pour into a spray bottle. Apply directly to the foliage of plants being targeted by pests. The spicy nature of the spray irritates pests, discouraging them from eating the plants. Use caution when applying, as pepper spray can be irritating to human skin and eyes as well.

Peppermint to Repel Mice

Peppermint is a natural and effective way to repel mice due to its strong scent, which mice find overwhelming. Plant peppermint around the perimeter of your garden or home, or use cotton balls soaked in peppermint oil in areas where mice are frequent. The intense aroma disrupts mice's olfactory senses, discouraging them from entering or lingering in the area. Regular applications of peppermint oil or fresh plantings of peppermint can help maintain its effectiveness as a repellent, providing a non-toxic and pleasant-smelling deterrent against rodent invasions.

Using plastic forks can be an innovative and harmless method to deter small animals from digging in your garden. Simply stick the forks into the soil with the tines pointing upward, spacing them closely enough to make it uncomfortable for animals such as squirrels and cats to step or dig around the plants. This physical barrier can protect seedlings and young plants from being disturbed or damaged by curious or hungry animals, without causing them harm. It's an inexpensive and straightforward solution that can be implemented quickly with materials often already available at home.

Rhubarb Leaf Pesticide

Rhubarb leaves contain oxalic acid, which can be used to make a natural pesticide. Although toxic if ingested by humans, when used as a spray, the natural compounds in rhubarb leaves can effectively target aphids and other pests. To prepare the spray, boil rhubarb leaves in water for about 20 minutes, strain the liquid, and let it cool. Once cooled, add a teaspoon of dish soap to help the mixture stick to plant leaves, and spray directly onto the affected plants. Use this pesticide cautiously, as the high concentration of oxalic acid can also affect plant health if overused.

Soap as a Deer Repellent

Using soap as a deer repellent is a simple and effective way to protect your garden. Hang bars of strongly scented soap from stakes or branches around the perimeter of your garden, or grate the soap and sprinkle it directly around plants. The strong scent of the soap is unappealing to deer and can mask the scent of your plants, discouraging deer from browsing. Replace the soap regularly to ensure it remains effective, especially after rain. This method is safe for the garden and the environment, offering a chemical-free alternative to traditional repellents.

Soap Pieces as Deer Repellent

Scattering soap pieces around your garden can serve as an effective deterrent against deer. The strong fragrance of the soap masks plant aromas that attract deer, thus keeping them away from your vegetation. Grate bars of pungent soap and distribute the shavings around the base of plants that are particularly vulnerable to deer. The scent will need to be maintained by periodically adding fresh soap, especially after rainfall, as the scent diminishes over time. This method is environmentally friendly and avoids the use of harsh chemicals, making it ideal for organic gardening practices.

Soap Spray for Insects

Soap spray is a safe and effective way to combat a variety of garden pests such as aphids, mites, and whiteflies. To create this spray, mix a few drops of mild liquid dish soap with water in a spray bottle. The soap works by breaking down the outer coating of pests, causing them to dehydrate and die. Spray directly onto affected plants, covering both the tops and undersides of leaves where insects tend to hide. This method is gentle on plants and the environment, making it a preferred choice for organic gardening. Be sure to test the spray on a small area first to ensure it does not damage the plants.

Soap Water for Leaf Miner Control

Soap water is an effective treatment for controlling leaf miners, which are larvae that tunnel into leaves, creating visible trails. Mix a solution of mild liquid soap with water and spray it onto the foliage of affected plants. The soap helps to suffocate the leaf miners without harming the plant. Regular applications may be necessary to manage these pests effectively. As always, test the soap solution on a small portion of the plant first to check for any adverse reactions.

Spice Mix to Repel Mammals

A spice mix containing strong-smelling substances like cayenne pepper, garlic powder, and cinnamon can be an effective repellent for various mammals such as deer, rabbits, and squirrels. These spices irritate the nasal passages of mammals, deterring them from nibbling on garden plants. To use, sprinkle the spice mix directly around the perimeter of the garden or near specific plants that require protection. Reapply regularly, especially after rainfall, to maintain its effectiveness. This method offers a natural, non-toxic way to protect your garden without harming wildlife.

Stale Bread Slug Trap

Stale bread can be used as an economical and simple trap for slugs. Place a piece of stale bread in a shallow dish and bury it slightly in the garden soil where slug activity is noted. The slugs are attracted to the yeast in the bread and will congregate beneath it. Check the trap the following morning and remove the slugs. This method provides a humane way to control slug populations, helping protect your plants from damage while using up kitchen scraps that might otherwise go to waste.

Sticky Tape for Flying Insects

Sticky tape is a straightforward and effective tool for controlling flying insects in and around the garden. These adhesive tapes can be hung or placed near plants that typically attract pests like whiteflies, aphids, and mosquitoes. The bright colors of the tape often attract insects, and once they land, they become trapped on the sticky surface. This method is especially useful in greenhouses or near house entrances, providing a chemical-free option to keep flying pests at bay. Regular replacement of the tape is necessary to maintain its effectiveness as it can quickly become covered with trapped insects.

Tobacco Spray for Pests

Tobacco spray is a traditional remedy used to combat a wide range of garden pests, including aphids, caterpillars, and leaf miners. To prepare the spray, soak tobacco leaves or cigarettes in water until the mixture becomes a light brown color. Strain the solution and add a small amount of dish soap to help the mixture adhere to plant leaves. Spray this solution directly onto the pests or affected areas of the plant, being cautious as tobacco spray can be potent and harmful to some plants. Always test a small area first and use sparingly, as nicotine is toxic and can affect plant health.

Wood Ash for Pest Control

Wood ash is a valuable by-product for garden pest control, offering a natural source of potassium and a deterrent against slugs and snails. Sprinkle wood ash directly around the base of plants, which creates a barrier that these pests avoid because of its dry, caustic nature. Additionally, wood ash can be used to raise the soil pH slightly, making it less hospitable for some soil-dwelling pests. However, use wood ash cautiously, especially in gardens with already alkaline soil, to avoid altering the soil chemistry too drastically. Regular application may be necessary to maintain its effectiveness as a pest deterrent.

CHAPTER 8: DISEASE MANAGEMENT

Managing plant diseases effectively is crucial for maintaining a healthy and productive garden. Diseases can swiftly spread through a garden, causing widespread damage and reducing yield. This section delves into a range of natural remedies and preventive measures that can help combat common plant diseases, minimizing the reliance on chemical fungicides and pesticides. Techniques such as using baking soda as a fungicide, applying cornmeal to combat fungus, and utilizing hydrogen peroxide for treating root rot provide gardeners with sustainable options for disease management. These methods not only help control existing infections but also enhance plant resilience against future outbreaks.

We also explore innovative approaches like the use of aspirin water to boost plant immunity, the application of neem oil for its antifungal properties, and the protective effects of chamomile tea on seedlings. Whether preventing mildew with apple cider vinegar or fighting black spot with baking powder, each strategy is designed to be environmentally friendly and easy to implement. By integrating these natural solutions into regular garden care, gardeners can protect their plants from diseases while fostering a healthier garden ecosystem. These methods align with organic gardening principles, prioritizing safety and sustainability without compromising plant health.

Apple Cider Vinegar for Mildew

Apple cider vinegar (ACV) is an effective organic remedy for combating powdery mildew on plants. The acidic nature of vinegar helps to alter the pH on the leaf surface, making it less hospitable for mildew spores to thrive. To use ACV as a mildew treatment, dilute it with water—typically one part vinegar to three parts water—and add a drop of liquid soap to help the solution adhere to the leaves. Spray this mixture onto affected plants, being careful to avoid direct sunlight hours to prevent leaf burn. Regular application can help control the spread of mildew and keep your plants healthy.

Aspirin Water for Disease Prevention

Aspirin water can bolster plant health and aid in preventing various diseases, including blight and fungal infections. Aspirin contains salicylic acid, which is known to trigger a plant's natural defense mechanisms against pathogens. To prepare aspirin water, dissolve one aspirin tablet (usually 325 mg) in a gallon of water and spray it onto your plants every two to three weeks. This preventative measure can enhance the immune response of plants, making them more resilient to disease attacks and environmental stresses.

Baking Powder for Black Spot

Baking powder is a useful fungicide for treating black spot, a common fungal disease that affects roses and other plants. The fungicidal properties of baking powder help to prevent the fungus from spreading and killing the plant tissues. Mix a tablespoon of baking powder with a liter of water and a few drops of liquid soap (to improve adherence to the leaf surfaces) and spray it on the affected leaves. Apply this solution weekly to control black spot outbreaks, ensuring to cover all affected areas thoroughly, as the disease can spread rapidly under favorable conditions.

Baking Soda Fungicide

Baking soda is a versatile household item that doubles as an effective fungicide against various fungal diseases, such as powdery mildew and other leaf spot diseases. Creating a baking soda spray involves mixing 1 tablespoon of baking soda with 1 gallon of water and a small amount of liquid soap to help the mixture stick to plant leaves. This solution, when sprayed on affected plants, creates an alkaline environment that inhibits fungal growth. Use this spray as a preventative measure and during early signs of fungal infection to protect your garden plants from significant damage.

Boric Acid for Plant Rot

Boric acid is an effective treatment for plant rot, particularly in cases where fungal infections are involved. It acts as both a fungicide and a bactericide, helping to halt the spread of rot within the plant. To use boric acid for plant rot, dissolve a small amount of boric acid powder in water and apply it directly to the affected areas of the plant. This treatment can be especially helpful for stem rot and root rot by targeting and eliminating the pathogens responsible. Care should be taken when applying boric acid as it can be toxic in high concentrations, so it's important to follow the recommended dilution rates closely.

Chamomile Tea for Mildew

Chamomile tea is a natural remedy known for its fungicidal properties, making it effective against mildew on plants. The antifungal compounds present in chamomile help prevent and treat mildew by inhibiting fungal growth. To use, brew a strong pot of chamomile tea, let it cool, and then spray it directly onto the leaves of affected plants. Regular applications can help manage mildew outbreaks and keep other fungal diseases at bay as well. This gentle, natural treatment is safe for most plants and beneficial for maintaining overall plant health.

Chamomile Tea for Seedlings

Chamomile tea is beneficial for seedlings, acting as a mild fungicide to prevent "damping off"—a fungal condition that causes seedlings to rot at the base. To protect your seedlings, water them with cooled chamomile tea periodically, using it as a substitute for regular watering once a week. The antifungal properties of chamomile help keep harmful pathogens in check, promoting stronger, healthier growth in young plants. This natural approach is gentle enough not to harm delicate seedlings while effectively safeguarding them from common fungal threats.

Cinnamon Fungicide

Cinnamon is known for its natural fungicidal properties and can be used to prevent and treat fungal infections in plants, such as root rot and damping off in seedlings. To create a cinnamon fungicide, sprinkle cinnamon powder directly on the soil around the base of the plants or on the affected areas of the plant. For a broader application, you can also make a cinnamon water spray by steeping cinnamon sticks in hot water, allowing it to cool, and then spraying the solution directly on the plants. Regular use of cinnamon can help suppress fungal growth and protect new plants from infection, making it a safe and aromatic addition to your plant care regimen.

Cornmeal as Fungicide

Cornmeal is an organic fungicide that can be effective against a variety of fungal diseases in plants, including root rot and dollar spot on lawns. The natural fungus-fighting compounds in cornmeal help inhibit the growth of certain pathogens when applied to the soil. To use cornmeal as a fungicide, sprinkle it directly around the base of affected plants or mix it into the top layer of soil. Alternatively, cornmeal can be soaked in water to create a "cornmeal tea," which can then be used to water plants, applying the fungicidal benefits directly to the root zone. This method is environmentally friendly and adds organic matter to the soil, promoting overall soil health.

Garlic and Pepper Disease Spray

Garlic and hot pepper spray is a powerful organic concoction used to deter pests and prevent fungal diseases. Both garlic and peppers contain compounds that are natural repellents and anti-fungal agents. To make this spray, blend a few cloves of garlic and one or two hot peppers with a pint of water, let it steep overnight, then strain and add a drop of dish soap to help the mixture adhere to plant leaves. Spray this solution on the foliage of plants that are susceptible to pests and diseases. The strong odors and tastes help keep a variety of insects at bay and can inhibit the growth of fungal spores on leaves.

Hydrogen Peroxide for Root Rot

Hydrogen peroxide is an effective treatment for root rot by providing oxygen to the soil and killing off anaerobic bacteria and fungi that thrive in oxygen-deprived environments. To treat root rot, dilute hydrogen peroxide with water (typically using a ratio of one part hydrogen peroxide to ten parts water) and drench the soil around the base of the affected plant. The solution will break down into water and oxygen, the latter of which helps to aerate the soil and revitalize sick roots. It's crucial to correctly diagnose root rot and use this treatment sparingly to avoid harming beneficial soil organisms.

Milk and Water for Viruses

A mixture of milk and water has been shown to help boost plant immunity and can be effective in preventing viral infections in plants, such as mosaic virus. The proteins in milk, when exposed to sunlight, produce free radicals that are believed to have antiviral properties. To use this remedy, mix one part milk with nine parts water and spray it on the plants every two weeks or so. This spray is particularly effective on cucurbits (like cucumbers and squash) and tomatoes, helping to reduce the incidence of viral diseases and promote healthier, more vigorous plants.

Milk Spray for Roses

Milk spray is a renowned natural remedy for managing fungal diseases such as powdery mildew on roses. The proteins and amino acids in milk react to sunlight, creating an antifungal effect that inhibits the growth of mildew. To prepare a milk spray, mix one part milk with two parts water and spray it onto the leaves of rose bushes, ensuring both the tops and undersides are covered. This treatment is most effective when applied weekly, especially during the morning, allowing the sun to activate the milk's protective properties. Regular use not only helps control fungal diseases but also enhances the overall vitality of the roses.

Mustard Seed Extract for Fungus

Mustard seed extract is an effective natural fungicide, particularly beneficial in combating root fungi and soil-borne pathogens. The bioactive compounds in mustard seeds act as a deterrent against fungal growth and help protect plants from various diseases. To use mustard seed extract, grind mustard seeds into a powder and steep them in hot water, allowing the mixture to cool before applying it to the soil around your plants. This treatment can help suppress fungal growth and boost plant defense mechanisms, contributing to healthier garden soil and stronger plants.

Neem Oil for Fungal Diseases

Neem oil is a potent organic treatment widely used to combat fungal diseases in plants, including rust, scab, and mildew. Derived from the seeds of the neem tree, it contains compounds that are both fungicidal and insecticidal. To apply, mix neem oil with water and a small amount of mild dish soap (which acts as an emulsifier) and spray it directly onto affected plant areas. Regular applications can effectively manage fungal infections and also deter various pests, making neem oil a versatile addition to garden pest and disease management practices.

Oat Tea for Plant Health

Oat tea can be used as a natural tonic to enhance plant health, thanks to the nutrients and minerals found in oats, such as potassium and magnesium. These nutrients support plant vigor and resilience against diseases. To make oat tea, soak oat grains or oat straw in water for several days, allowing the nutrients to leach into the liquid. Strain the mixture and use the tea to water your plants, providing them with a nourishing boost that promotes strong growth and vitality. This simple yet effective remedy is particularly useful for young seedlings and plants that appear nutrient-deficient.

More Disease Management Secrets

Secret	Why It Works	What to Do
Yogurt Spray	Contains beneficial bacteria that help fight fungal infections and promote plant health.	Mix plain yogurt with water (1:1 ratio) and spray onto plant leaves to combat powdery mildew and other fungal diseases.
Aloe Vera Juice	Enhances plant immunity and helps in healing plant wounds.	Mix aloe vera juice with water (1:10 ratio) and spray onto plants to boost their immune system and treat damaged tissues.
Tobacco Tea	Acts as a natural fungicide and insect repellent.	Soak tobacco leaves in water for a day, strain, and spray the solution onto plants to protect against fungal infections and pests.
Horseradish Root	Contains natural antibacterial and antifungal properties.	Crush horseradish root and mix with water, strain, and spray onto plants to treat bacterial and fungal diseases.
Eucalyptus Oil Spray	Has antifungal and antibacterial properties that protect plants from diseases.	Mix a few drops of eucalyptus oil with water and a drop of dish soap, then spray onto plant leaves.
Willow Bark Tea	Contains salicylic acid, which boosts plant immunity.	Boil willow bark in water, let it cool, and use the tea to water plants or spray onto leaves to enhance disease resistance.
Ginger Root Extract	Acts as a natural antifungal agent.	Crush ginger root, mix with water, strain, and spray onto plants to prevent fungal infections.
Rosemary Oil Spray	Has antifungal and antibacterial properties that protect plants.	Mix a few drops of rosemary oil with water and a drop of dish soap, then spray onto plant leaves.
Clove Oil Fungicide	Contains eugenol, which is effective in treating fungal diseases.	Mix a few drops of clove oil with water and a drop of dish soap, then spray onto affected plants.
Onion Juice	Has natural antifungal and antibacterial properties.	Extract juice from onions, dilute with water, and spray onto plants to treat and prevent diseases.
Apple Cider Vinegar	Alters the pH on the leaf surface, making it less hospitable for fungal spores.	Dilute one part apple cider vinegar with three parts water and spray onto affected plant leaves.
Garlic Infusion	Contains sulfur compounds that have antifungal and antibacterial properties.	Crush garlic cloves, soak in water overnight, strain, and spray the solution onto plants.
Corn Starch Solution	Helps in treating fungal diseases by creating a barrier on plant surfaces.	Mix corn starch with water to form a paste, dilute with more water, and spray onto plants.
Peppermint Tea Spray	Acts as a natural fungicide and insect repellent.	Brew peppermint tea, let it cool, and spray onto plants to protect against diseases and pests.

CHAPTER 9: SEASONAL GARDENING WISDOM

Seasonal gardening requires a deep understanding of how the shifting weather and varying conditions affect plant growth and garden maintenance. Each season brings its unique challenges and opportunities, requiring specific strategies and adjustments to ensure garden health and productivity. For instance, hot weather watering techniques are crucial in the summer to prevent dehydration and heat stress, while autumn leaf mulching provides essential nutrients and insulation for soil as temperatures drop. Understanding these seasonal nuances allows gardeners to optimize their practices, from planting and pruning to protection and pest management.

The knowledge of how to adapt gardening techniques to seasonal changes is invaluable. For example, using burlap sacks for frost protection in the winter can save sensitive plants, and planning spring bulbs in the fall ensures vibrant early blooms. This chapter explores various essential seasonal practices, such as reflective mulch to cool plants in summer, the benefits of seasonal mulching, and the establishment of pollinator gardens that thrive during specific times of the year. Additionally, practices like winter indoor edible gardening extend the growing season, allowing gardeners to enjoy fresh produce year-round. By aligning gardening practices with the rhythms of nature, one can achieve a flourishing garden that responds gracefully to the Earth's cycles.

Autumn Leaf Mulching

Autumn leaf mulching is a beneficial practice that recycles fallen leaves into a valuable garden resource, providing insulation, moisture retention, and nutrient enrichment to the soil as they decompose. Instead of discarding the leaves collected during fall cleanup, gardeners can spread them over garden beds or around trees and shrubs. This natural mulch layer protects plant roots from winter cold and temperature fluctuations, while also suppressing weed growth and slowly releasing organic matter back into the soil. The process not only enhances soil health and fertility but also reduces the need for additional fertilizers and water, making it an environmentally friendly choice that enhances the sustainability of garden ecosystems.

Burlap Sack Frost Protection

Burlap sacks provide an effective and eco-friendly method for protecting plants from frost damage during cold snaps. The breathable fabric allows for air circulation while still insulating plants from harsh temperatures. Gardeners can drape burlap sacks over vulnerable plants or wrap them around the bases to shield them from frost. This method is particularly useful for tender perennials or newly planted shrubs that might not withstand sudden drops in temperature. Using burlap is also advantageous as it can be easily removed during warmer days to prevent overheating and then replaced as temperatures drop again.

Burlap Wrap for Tree Protection

Burlap wrap is commonly used to protect trees from winter damage, including frost bites and the harsh effects of windburn. Wrapping the burlap around the trunk and extending it to the lower branches helps to insulate the tree without trapping moisture, thereby preventing bark and tissue damage that can occur during the cold months. This protection is particularly important for young trees or those with thin bark that are more susceptible to winter stresses. Burlap is also a preferred material due to its breathability, ensuring that the covered parts of the tree do not succumb to mold or fungus.

Fall Garden Cleanup

Fall garden cleanup is essential for maintaining plant health and preparing the garden for the coming spring. This process involves removing dead or diseased plant material, which could harbor pests and diseases over the winter. Gardeners should also cut back perennials, rake up leaves, and compost any organic waste that is not infected. Additionally, cleaning up the garden in the fall can help to reduce the likelihood of pest infestations and gives the gardener a cleaner slate for planting and maintenance activities in the spring. This seasonal tidying not only keeps the garden looking neat but also promotes healthier growth and development in the next growing season.

Hot Weather Watering

Watering in hot weather is critical to ensure that plants remain hydrated and healthy during periods of intense heat and sunlight. During these times, it's important to water deeply and less frequently, encouraging roots to grow deeper into the soil where moisture lasts longer. Early morning is the best time to water, as it reduces evaporation and allows water to seep into the soil before temperatures peak. Additionally, using methods such as drip irrigation or soaker hoses can be very effective, as they deliver water directly to the base of the plant, minimizing waste and maximizing moisture absorption. Proper hot weather watering techniques are essential for preventing stress, conserving water, and maintaining a thriving garden even under challenging conditions.

Planting by Moon Phases

Planting by moon phases is an age-old practice that many gardeners follow, based on the belief that the lunar cycle affects plant growth. The waxing phase, when the moon is increasing in light, is said to be ideal for planting above-ground crops due to increased moisture retention in the soil, enhancing seed germination and root development. Conversely, the waning moon, when it decreases in light, is believed to be best for planting root crops, as gravitational pull is lower, which is thought to encourage root growth. While scientific support for this method varies, many gardeners swear by its effectiveness and integrate it into their seasonal planting strategies for optimizing crop yields.

Reflective Mulch

Reflective mulch is used in gardens to improve light exposure to plants and manage pests. This type of mulch is made from a reflective material, such as metallic plastic, that reflects sunlight up onto the undersides of leaves, which can help enhance photosynthesis, particularly in shaded areas or dense gardens. Additionally, the increased light can disorient and repel certain pests, such as aphids and whiteflies, which are less likely to settle on plants that are brightly illuminated. Reflective mulch is particularly useful during the growing season when sunlight is crucial for optimal growth and when pest pressure is high.

Seasonal Mulching

Seasonal mulching involves adapting mulch application according to the changing weather conditions throughout the year to protect and nurture plants. In the spring, a lighter mulch can be applied to warm the soil and encourage early growth. During the hot summer months, a thicker layer of mulch helps retain soil moisture and keep roots cool. In autumn, mulch can be refreshed to protect plant roots from the cold and suppress weed growth, while winter mulch is important for insulating perennial and sensitive plants against freezing temperatures. Each seasonal application ensures that plants receive the best possible protection and support for their specific growth phases.

Seasonal Pollinator Gardens

Seasonal pollinator gardens are designed to provide year-round support for pollinators such as bees, butterflies, and hummingbirds. By selecting a variety of plants that bloom at different times of the year, gardeners can ensure a continuous supply of nectar and pollen. Such gardens not only support the health and populations of local pollinator species but also enhance garden productivity by ensuring that flowering plants are adequately pollinated. Planting diverse species also promotes greater ecological balance, attracting beneficial insects that contribute to pest control and overall garden health.

Spring Bulb Planning

Planning for spring bulbs involves selecting and planting bulbs in the fall before the ground freezes. This timing allows the bulbs to establish roots and undergo the necessary cold dormancy period before spring. Choices might include tulips, daffodils, hyacinths, and crocuses, which are popular for their vibrant colors and early blooms. Strategic planning involves considering bloom times to achieve a succession of colors and interest throughout the spring season. Proper depth and spacing are crucial for optimal growth, as is choosing a planting site with adequate drainage and sufficient sunlight. Spring bulb planning is a hopeful garden activity that sets the stage for a lively and colorful garden as winter fades.

Summer Pruning Techniques

Summer pruning is a crucial technique for managing plant health and enhancing fruit and flower production. Unlike spring pruning, which focuses on removing dead or diseased wood, summer pruning helps control plant size, shape, and directs energy into fewer, higher quality fruits or more robust blooms. Techniques include thinning out new growth to ensure adequate air circulation and light penetration within the plant. For fruit trees, summer pruning can also help reduce the risk of diseases and pest infestations by removing parts that are overly dense or that show signs of infection. This seasonal pruning ensures plants remain vibrant and productive during their active growing period.

Winter Indoor Edibles

Growing edibles indoors during the winter provides a fresh supply of herbs and vegetables, bridging the gap left by the dormant outdoor garden. Options for indoor cultivation include herbs like basil and parsley, leafy greens like spinach and arugula, and even dwarf varieties of vegetables like tomatoes and peppers. Using containers or hydroponic systems, gardeners can maintain a controlled environment with sufficient lighting, either through sunny windowsills or supplemental grow lights, and consistent temperatures. This method not only extends the growing season but also brings greenery and vitality into the home during the colder months.

Winter Plant Protection

Winter plant protection is essential to shield sensitive plants from freezing temperatures, frost, and harsh conditions. Techniques include mulching around the base of plants to insulate roots, using burlap wraps or frost cloths to shield above-ground parts, and constructing windbreaks or shelters for particularly vulnerable species. For potted plants, moving them indoors or into a frost-free greenhouse can provide the necessary warmth and protection. These measures help ensure that plants survive the winter with minimal stress, ready to resume active growth in the spring. Implementing these strategies is a proactive approach to garden maintenance that preserves the health and beauty of the landscape through the toughest months of the year.

FINAL THOUGHTS AND FUTURE GROWTH

As we conclude this journey through the depths of traditional and often forgotten gardening wisdom, it's clear that the secrets shared offer more than just tips—they provide a foundation for transforming your gardening practices. This book has meticulously compiled over 180 invaluable insights that span a diverse range of topics, each meticulously designed to help you achieve a more bountiful harvest and create an effortlessly thriving garden. From the symbiotic strategies of companion gardening to the preventive measures of disease management, each category has been crafted to enhance your understanding and application of time-tested gardening methods.

In chapters covering Fertilization and Soil Health, you've learned how to enrich your garden naturally, promoting vibrant plant growth. Garden Planning and Design offered innovative techniques for maximizing both the aesthetic and functional aspects of your space. The Pest Control and Weed Prevention and Removal chapters equipped you with natural solutions to keep unwanted visitors at bay without resorting to harsh chemicals. Plant Care and Maintenance provided insights into the daily requirements of garden upkeep, ensuring your plants receive the best care. Seasonal Gardening Wisdom emphasized the importance of timing and adaptability, teaching you how to work harmoniously with nature's cycles. Finally, Water Management explored efficient techniques to conserve one of our most precious resources, ensuring your garden remains sustainable in all environmental conditions.

By integrating these age-old secrets into your gardening practice, you are not only enhancing your own gardening experience but also contributing to a more sustainable and ecologically friendly world. Whether you are a novice gardener or a seasoned green thumb, the lessons encapsulated in this book are designed to foster a deeper connection with the earth and inspire a richer, more rewarding gardening adventure.